TRANSMATH®

Making Sense of Rational Numbers

Interactive Text

John Woodward
Mary Stroh

Cambium
LEARNING® Group | Voyager
LEARNING

13 14 15 16 17   B&B   17 16 15 14 13

ISBN 13: 978-160697-044-7
ISBN: 1-60697-044-5

181999/6-13

Printed in the United States of America
Published and distributed by

17855 Dallas Parkway • Suite 400 • Dallas, Texas 75287 • 1-800-547-6747
www.voyagerlearning.com

TABLE OF CONTENTS

Name _____ Date _____

 Skills Maintenance
Multiplying by 10

Activity 1

Solve.

1. $1 \cdot 10$ _____

2. $10 \cdot 8$ _____

3. $10 \cdot 10$ _____

4. $10 \cdot 9$ _____

5. $10 \cdot 5$ _____

6. $10 \cdot 6$ _____

7. $4 \cdot 10$ _____

8. $3 \cdot 10$ _____

9. $10 \cdot 2$ _____

Name _____ Date _____

%÷ Apply Skills
Whole Numbers and Powers of 10

Activity 1

Tell the value of the underlined digit in each number.

1. 43,0<u>9</u>1 _____

2. 1,<u>0</u>01 _____

3. 4,<u>9</u>80,721 _____

4. 7<u>0</u>3 _____

5. 5,<u>9</u>80,092 _____

6. <u>7</u>,736,078 _____

Activity 2

Fill in the missing information in the power-of-10 table. The first one is done for you.

	_____ · 10	_____ · 100	_____ · 1,000
7,000	700 · 10	70 · 100	7 · 1,000
8,000			
	200 · 10		
5,000			
		60 · 100	
			9 · 1,000

Name _____ Date _____

Problem-Solving Activity
Reading Data in Graphs

Let's imagine that the company that studied the decline in newspaper subscribers also looked at the number of people in the community who subscribed to magazines. Here are the data for four years. To make the data easier to graph, the numbers are rounded.

Year 1: 95,000 magazine subscribers
Year 2: 100,000 magazine subscribers
Year 3: 92,000 magazine subscribers
Year 4: 105,000 magazine subscribers

Make a bar graph that shows the change in the number of magazine subscribers over the four years. Be sure to include labels and a title on your graph.

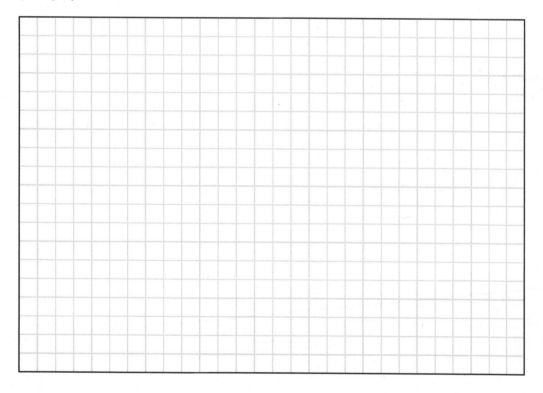

mBook Reinforce Understanding
Use the mBook *Study Guide* to review lesson concepts.

Name _____ Date _____

 Skills Maintenance
Mixed Operations With Tens

> **Activity 1**

Solve.

1. 40
    − 30

2. 50
    − 20

3. 70
    + 10

4. 60
    + 80

5. 20
    × 3

6. 60
    × 4

Name _____ Date _____

 Apply Skills
Operations and Whole Numbers

Activity 1

Solve the problems first using the traditional method and then using partial product.

	Traditional	**Partial Product**

1. $\begin{array}{r} 312 \\ \times \quad 2 \\ \hline \end{array}$

2. $\begin{array}{r} 547 \\ \times \quad 9 \\ \hline \end{array}$

3. $\begin{array}{r} 601 \\ \times \quad 8 \\ \hline \end{array}$

4. $\begin{array}{r} 709 \\ \times \quad 7 \\ \hline \end{array}$

Name _____ Date _____

Problem-Solving Activity
Horizontal Bar Graphs

Make a horizontal bar graph using the data in the table. The graph should show how fast five people ran in a 400-meter race. The time for each racer is given in seconds. Be sure to put labels and a title in the right places on your graph.

Racer	Time in Seconds
Jimenez	85
Schwartz	105
Mingas	80
Johnson	90
Tegalo	95

mBook **Reinforce Understanding**
Use the mBook *Study Guide* to review lesson concepts.

Name _____ Date _____

Skills Maintenance
Operations With Whole Numbers

Activity 1

Solve.

1.   368
    + 295

2.   483
    − 163

3.   568
    ×   4

4. 9)972

Name _____ Date _____

%÷= Apply Skills
Whole Numbers, Fractions, and Decimal Numbers

Activity 1

Fill in the missing decimal numbers and fractions on the number lines.

1.

2.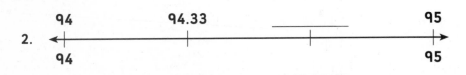

3.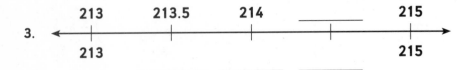

4.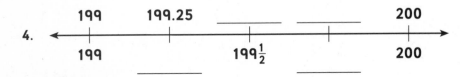

Activity 2

Circle the larger fraction or decimal number.

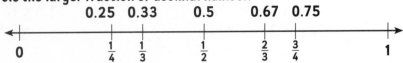

1. Which is larger?   (circle one) $\frac{1}{3}$ or $\frac{1}{2}$

2. Which is larger?   (circle one)   0.33   or   0.25

3. Which is larger?   (circle one) $\frac{3}{4}$ or $\frac{1}{3}$

4. Which is larger?   (circle one)   0.5   or   0.75

Name _____ Date _____

 ### Problem-Solving Activity
Vertical Bar Graphs

Survey your class. Then make a vertical bar graph based on that information. Be sure to add labels and a title.

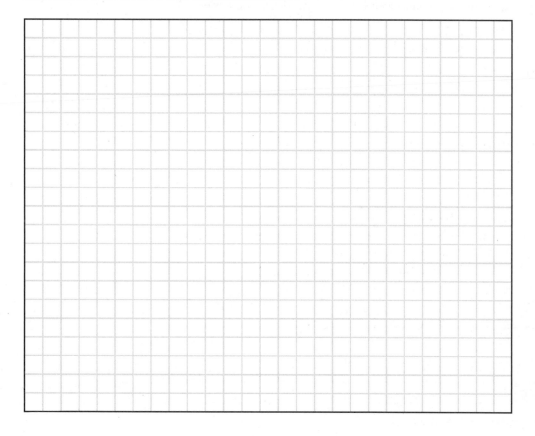

mBook **Reinforce Understanding**
Use the mBook *Study Guide* to review lesson concepts.

Name _____ Date _____

 ## Skills Maintenance
Fractions and Decimal Numbers on the Number Line

Activity 1

Fill in the missing decimal numbers and fractions on the number lines.

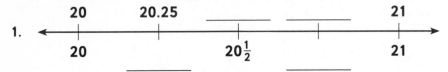

1.

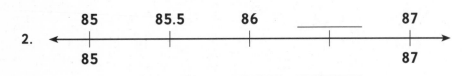

2.

3.

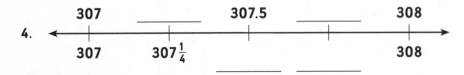

4.

Activity 2

Circle the larger fraction or decimal number.

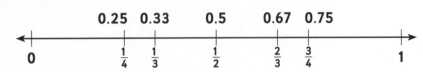

1. Which is larger? (circle one) $\frac{2}{3}$ or $\frac{1}{2}$

2. Which is larger? (circle one)   0.66   or   0.25

3. Which is larger? (circle one)   0.5   or   0.25

4. Which is larger? (circle one) $\frac{1}{3}$ or $\frac{1}{4}$

Name _____ Date _____

 Apply Skills
Equivalent Fractions

Activity 1

Fill in the blank to make an equal fraction. Then divide and shade the fraction bar to show the equal fraction.

1. $\dfrac{2}{3} = \dfrac{}{6}$

$\dfrac{2}{3}$

$\dfrac{}{6}$

2. $\dfrac{1}{4} = \dfrac{}{8}$

$\dfrac{1}{4}$

$\dfrac{}{8}$

3. $\dfrac{2}{5} = \dfrac{}{10}$

$\dfrac{2}{5}$

$\dfrac{}{10}$

4. $\dfrac{4}{8} = \dfrac{}{2}$

$\dfrac{4}{8}$

$\dfrac{}{2}$

Name _____ Date _____

Problem-Solving Activity
Interpreting a List of Data

Read the problem and use the table of data to create a stem-and-leaf plot.

Scientists in New Mexico wanted to know how many bats slept in a small cave every day, so each day for a week they went inside the cave and counted them. The number of bats they counted is shown in the table. Use the data to make a stem-and-leaf plot of the number of bats counted.

Number of Bats in Pericote Pequeño Cave	
Monday	47
Tuesday	11
Wednesday	55
Thursday	38
Friday	98
Saturday	10
Sunday	24

Tens	Ones

mBook Reinforce Understanding
Use the mBook *Study Guide* to review lesson concepts.

Name _____ Date _____

 Skills Maintenance
Fractions

Activity 1

Write the fraction for each fraction bar. Then answer the question about it.

1. What is the fraction? _____ What is the denominator? _____

2. What is the fraction? _____ What is the numerator? _____

3. What is the fraction? _____ What are the total parts? _____

4. What is the fraction? _____ What are the parts we have? _____

Activity 2

Tell which fraction is larger by shading the fraction bars.

1. Which fraction is larger $\frac{1}{2}$ or $\frac{1}{4}$? _____

2. Which fraction is larger $\frac{2}{3}$ or $\frac{1}{2}$? _____

Name _____ Date _____

Apply Skills
Finding Equivalent Fractions

Activity 1

Divide each of the drawings to make equivalent fractions.

1. Use the drawing to show that $\frac{1}{2} = \frac{2}{4}$.

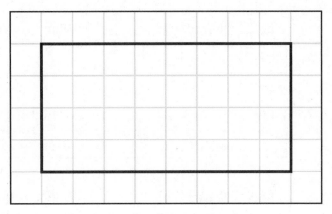

2. Use the drawing to show that $\frac{2}{3} = \frac{4}{6}$.

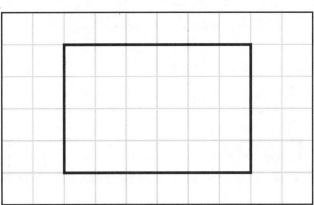

3. Use the drawing to show that $\frac{3}{4} = \frac{6}{8}$.

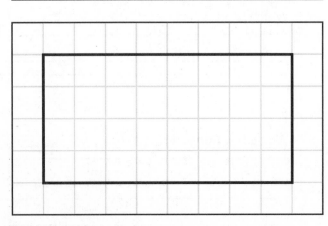

Name _____ Date _____

 Problem-Solving Activity
Line Graphs

The table and line graph show the outside temperature measured each hour during the afternoon. Answer the questions about them.

1. For how many hours does the line graph show data?

_____

2. What is the scale of the graph?

_____

3. What is the highest temperature recorded on the graph?

_____

4. What is the lowest temperature recorded on the graph?

_____

5. What trend does the graph show?

_____

Time	Temperature (in degrees)
12:00 PM	87
1:00 PM	89
2:00 PM	88
3:00 PM	82
4:00 PM	75
5:00 PM	70
6:00 PM	72
7:00 PM	70
8:00 PM	66

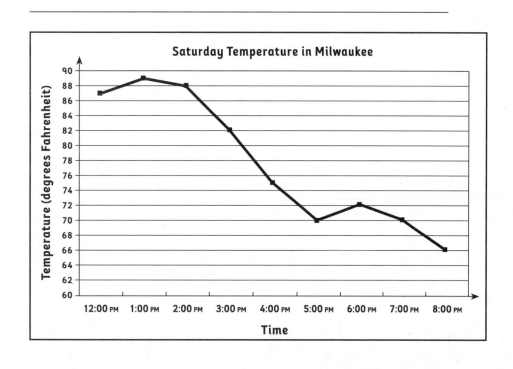

Name _____ Date _____

Skills Maintenance
Fractions

Activity 1

Circle the pairs of fraction bars that line up to make equivalent fractions.

Activity 2

Write the fraction for each fraction bar. Then answer the question.

1. What is the fraction? _____ What are the parts we have? _____

2. What is the fraction? _____ What is the denominator? _____

3. What is the fraction? _____ What is the numerator? _____

4. What is the fraction? _____ What is the denominator? _____

5. What is the fraction? _____ What are the parts we have? _____

Name _____ Date _____

Apply Skills
Adding and Subtracting Fractions

Activity 1

Solve the addition and subtraction problems using fraction bars.

1. $\frac{1}{2} + \frac{1}{5} =$ _____

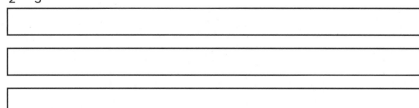

Rewrite _____

2. $\frac{1}{2} - \frac{1}{3} =$ _____

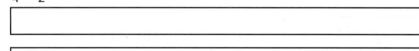

Rewrite _____

3. $\frac{1}{4} + \frac{1}{2} =$ _____

Rewrite _____

Name _____ Date _____

📝 Problem-Solving Activity
Making a Line Graph

The students in one science class studied how a tennis ball bounces. They measured the height of the bounces when the ball was dropped from the height of 20 feet. They kept track of how high the ball bounced for 10 bounces. Here is what they found.

Make a line graph that shows the height of the ball for the 10 bounces. Be sure to label your graph.

Bounce	Height
1st bounce	12 feet
2nd bounce	10 feet
3rd bounce	11 feet
4th bounce	10 feet
5th bounce	8 feet
6th bounce	6 feet
7th bounce	5 feet
8th bounce	4 feet
9th bounce	2 feet
10th bounce	1 foot

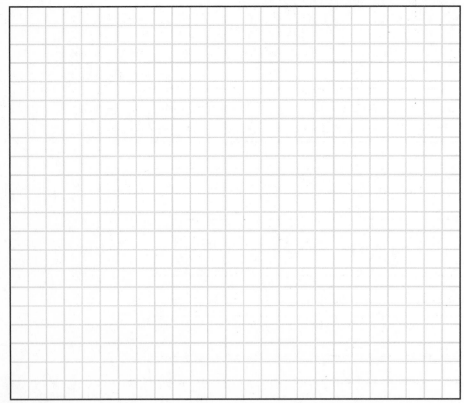

mBook Reinforce Understanding
Use the mBook *Study Guide* to review lesson concepts.

Name _____ Date _____

 ## Skills Maintenance
Multiplication Facts

Activity 1

Solve the multiplication facts.

1. 2 · 8 _____

2. 3 · 9 _____

3. 4 · 3 _____

4. 4 · 7 _____

5. 5 · 6 _____

6. 9 · 8 _____

7. 6 · 8 _____

8. 4 · 9 _____

9. 8 · 8 _____

Name _____ Date _____

%÷ Apply Skills
Multiplying Fractions by a Fraction Equal to 1

Activity 1

Fill in the missing numbers to make equivalent fractions.

1. $\dfrac{7}{10} \cdot \dfrac{\ \ }{\ \ } = \dfrac{\ \ }{30}$

2. $\dfrac{4}{8} \cdot \dfrac{\ \ }{\ \ } = \dfrac{\ \ }{16}$

3. $\dfrac{5}{9} \cdot \dfrac{\ \ }{\ \ } = \dfrac{\ \ }{27}$

4. $\dfrac{2}{4} \cdot \dfrac{\ \ }{\ \ } = \dfrac{\ \ }{8}$

5. $\dfrac{7}{10} \cdot \dfrac{\ \ }{\ \ } = \dfrac{\ \ }{40}$

6. $\dfrac{2}{5} \cdot \dfrac{\ \ }{\ \ } = \dfrac{\ \ }{10}$

Activity 2

Use fraction bars to show equivalent fractions. Divide the fraction bar and shade it.

1. $\dfrac{2}{5} = \dfrac{\ \ }{10}$

$\dfrac{2}{5}$

$\dfrac{\ \ }{10}$

2. $\dfrac{1}{3} = \dfrac{\ \ }{9}$

$\dfrac{1}{3}$

$\dfrac{\ \ }{9}$

3. $\dfrac{3}{4} = \dfrac{\ \ }{12}$

$\dfrac{3}{4}$

$\dfrac{\ \ }{12}$

4. $\dfrac{3}{4} = \dfrac{\ \ }{8}$

$\dfrac{3}{4}$

$\dfrac{\ \ }{8}$

Name _____ Date _____

 Skills Maintenance
Multiplication Facts

Activity 1

Solve the multiplication facts.

1. 2 · 8 _____

2. 3 · 8 _____

3. 4 · 8 _____

4. 5 · 8 _____

5. 3 · 9 _____

6. 4 · 9 _____

7. 5 · 9 _____

8. 6 · 9 _____

9. 5 · 7 _____

10. 6 · 7 _____

11. 7 · 7 _____

12. 8 · 7 _____

Name _____ Date _____

Apply Skills
Finding Common Denominators

Activity 1

Use the number lines to find common denominators. Then solve the problems.

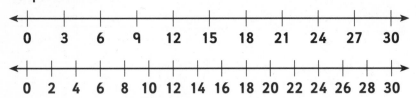

1. $\frac{1}{3} + \frac{1}{2}$ _____

2. $\frac{2}{3} - \frac{1}{2}$ _____

3. $\frac{2}{3} + \frac{1}{2}$ _____

4. $\frac{1}{2} - \frac{1}{3}$ _____

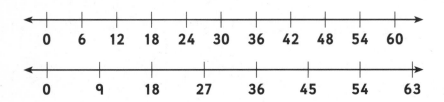

5. $\frac{1}{6} + \frac{1}{9}$ _____

6. $\frac{2}{9} - \frac{1}{6}$ _____

7. $\frac{2}{6} + \frac{1}{9}$ _____

8. $\frac{1}{6} - \frac{1}{9}$ _____

Name _____ Date _____

 Problem-Solving Activity
Two-Line Graphs

Make a line graph with two lines to show the data. Be sure to include labels
at the bottom and on the side of the graphs, as well as a title at the top.

Normal High Temperatures for Juneau, Alaska and Phoenix, Arizona in Degrees Fahrenheit					
	January	**February**	**March**	**April**	**May**
Juneau	30	34	40	48	55
Phoenix	65	70	75	85	95

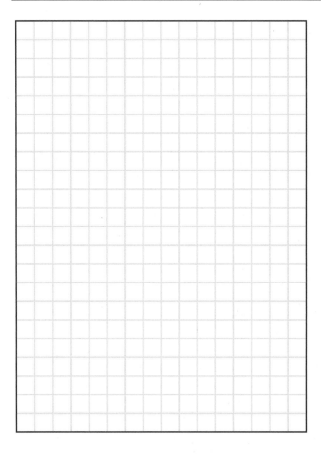

mBook **Reinforce Understanding**
Use the mBook *Study Guide* to review lesson concepts.

Name _____ Date _____

 Skills Maintenance
Multiplication Facts

Activity 1

Solve the multiplication facts.

1. 2 · 5 _____   2. 3 · 5 _____   3. 4 · 5 _____

4. 5 · 5 _____   5. 3 · 6 _____   6. 4 · 6 _____

7. 5 · 6 _____   8. 6 · 6 _____   9. 5 · 3 _____

10. 6 · 3 _____   11. 7 · 3 _____   12. 8 · 3 _____

Fractions

Activity 2

Write the fraction represented by the shaded part of the shapes.

1. What is the fraction? _____

2. What is the fraction? _____

3. What is the fraction? _____

4. What is the fraction? _____

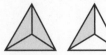

Name _____ Date _____

Apply Skills
The Least Common Multiple

Activity 1

Use the number lines to find the least common multiple.

1. 10 and 4 _____

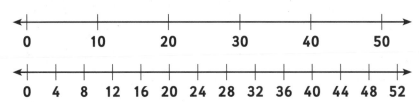

2. 7 and 3 _____

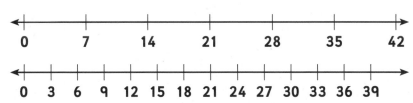

3. 6 and 8 _____

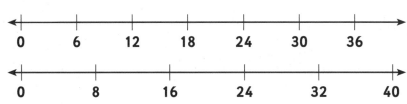

4. 5 and 7 _____

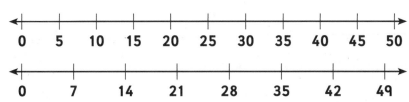

5. 4 and 9 _____

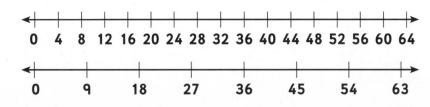

Name _____ Date _____

Problem-Solving Activity
Reading Line Graphs

The graph shows changes over time in the price of three different fruits. The prices could increase or decrease for many reasons. For example, the temperature might be too hot or too cold, or there might be too much or not enough rainfall. Read the graph carefully and answer the questions.

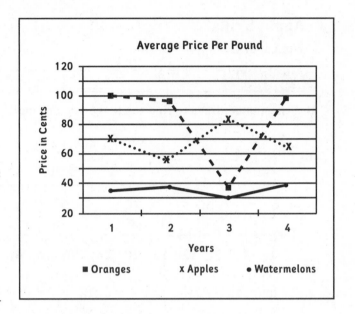

1. Which of the three fruits experienced the most changes (up or down) in price over the three years?

   _____

2. About what was the difference in price between watermelons and oranges in Year 2?

   _____

3. Which two fruits were about the same price per pound at one point in time?

   _____

4. Which fruit changed the least in price per pound from Year 1 to year 4?

   _____

5. About what was the difference in the price per pound of oranges and apples in Year 3?

   _____

6. Which of the three fruits changed the most in price between two years.

   _____

mBook **Reinforce Understanding**
Use the mBook *Study Guide* to review lesson concepts.

Name _____ Date _____

 Skills Maintenance
Multiplication Facts

Activity 1

Solve the multiplication facts.

1. 2 · 3 _____
2. 3 · 3 _____
3. 4 · 3 _____

4. 5 · 3 _____
5. 3 · 4 _____
6. 4 · 4 _____

7. 5 · 4 _____
8. 6 · 4 _____
9. 5 · 5 _____

10. 6 · 5 _____
11. 7 · 5 _____
12. 8 · 5 _____

Fractions

Activity 2

Write the fraction represented by the shaded part of the shapes.

1. What is the fraction? _____

2. What is the fraction? _____

3. What is the fraction? _____

Name _____ Date _____

Apply Skills
Adding Three Fractions

Activity 1

Solve. Rewrite the fractions with common denominators before solving.

1. $\frac{1}{6} + \frac{1}{9} + \frac{2}{3}$ _____

Rewrite _____

2. $\frac{3}{4} + \frac{1}{2} + \frac{1}{3}$ _____

Rewrite _____

3. $\frac{1}{4} + \frac{3}{6} + \frac{1}{8}$ _____

Rewrite _____

4. $\frac{1}{4} + \frac{1}{5} + \frac{1}{2}$ _____

Rewrite _____

Name _____ Date _____

Problem-Solving Activity
Choosing the Best Graph

Tell which graph you would use to display the data.

1. The number of people who voted for each candidate in an election

    _____

2. The time when the sun sets each day in a year

    _____

3. The number of different types of cupcakes sold at the school bake sale

    _____

4. The different distances students live from school

    _____

5. The average number of students who ride the bus in each grade

    _____

6. A track star's mile time over a season

    _____

7. The average number of books from each genre in the school library

    _____

8. The number wins each football team had in your district

    _____

9. The number of different types of dishes sold at a restaurant in a week

    _____

mBook Reinforce Understanding
Use the mBook *Study Guide* to review lesson concepts.

Name _____   Date _____

 Skills Maintenance
Multiplication Facts

Activity 1

Solve the multiplication facts.

1. 2 · 2 _____
2. 3 · 2 _____
3. 4 · 2 _____

4. 5 · 2 _____
5. 3 · 8 _____
6. 4 · 8 _____

7. 5 · 8 _____
8. 6 · 8 _____
9. 5 · 9 _____

10. 6 · 9 _____
11. 7 · 9 _____
12. 8 · 9 _____

Fractions

Activity 2

Tell what fraction is represented by each set of shapes. Then answer the question about each fraction.

1. What is the fraction? _____   What is the denominator? _____

2. What is the fraction? _____   What is the numerator? _____

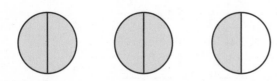

3. What is the fraction? _____   What are the total parts? _____

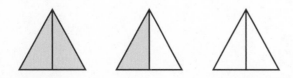

Name _____ Date _____

 Apply Skills
Does the Answer Make Sense?

Activity 1

Each of the problems has been solved incorrectly. Use fraction bars, number lines, and number sense to explain what is wrong.

1. $\frac{4}{5} + \frac{1}{5} = \frac{5}{10}$

What is the error?

_____

_____

2. $\frac{3}{4} - \frac{1}{2} = \frac{2}{2}$

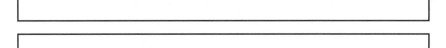

What is the error?

_____

_____

Name _____ Date _____

 Problem-Solving Activity
Which Graph Is Best?

Your boss wants you to create a graph of the number of people who came to the pool during the month. She doesn't really care about the temperature information. Choose the graph that works best for this information. Explain why you chose your graph.

Date	High Temperature for the Day	Number of People Who Came to the Pool
July 1	75	650
July 8	98	825
July 15	90	750
July 22	82	625
July 29	93	790

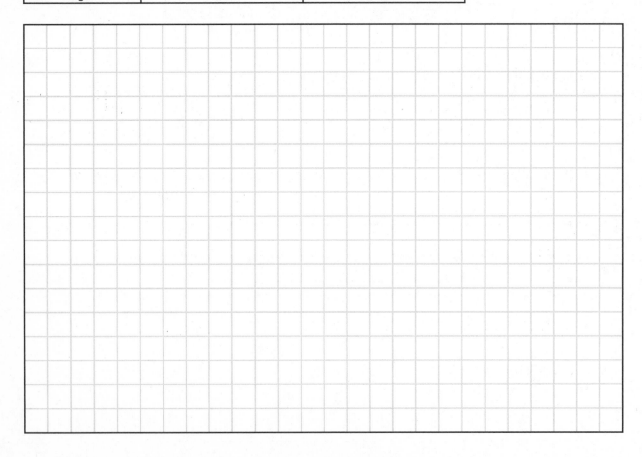

_____

_____

Name _____ Date _____

 Skills Maintenance
Multiplication

Activity 1

Solve the multiplication facts.

1. 6 · 7 _____
2. 2 · 9 _____
3. 11 · 4 _____

4. 3 · 10 _____
5. 5 · 6 _____
6. 7 · 8 _____

7. 10 · 10 _____
8. 4 · 4 _____
9. 7 · 2 _____

10. 3 · 6 _____
11. 9 · 5 _____
12. 8 · 4 _____

Fractions

Activity 2

Show the fractions using shapes, fraction bars, or number lines.

1. $\frac{7}{6}$
2. $\frac{10}{10}$

3. $\frac{5}{9}$
4. $\frac{2}{7}$

5. $\frac{6}{2}$
6. $\frac{8}{3}$

Name _____ Date _____

Unit Review
Whole Numbers and Fractions

Activity 1

Write the value of the underlined digit in each number.

1. 3_4_,890 _____

2. 564,_7_22 _____

3. _1_0,999,632 _____

4. 366,7_2_0,540 _____

Activity 2

Fill in the missing fractions and decimal numbers. Write the decimal numbers above the number line and the fractions below the number line.

1.

2.

3.

4.

Name _____ Date _____

Activity 3

Draw the fractions using shapes or fraction bars.

1. $\frac{3}{4}$ ☐☐ ☐☐ 2. $\frac{5}{4}$ ☐ ☐

3. $\frac{3}{2}$ ⬡ ⬡ 4. $\frac{3}{3}$ ▭

Activity 4

Tell which fraction is larger.

1. Which fraction is larger $\frac{5}{6}$ or $\frac{1}{3}$? _____

2. Which fraction is larger $\frac{12}{10}$ or $\frac{4}{7}$? _____

3. Which fraction is larger $\frac{6}{7}$ or $\frac{9}{9}$? _____

Activity 5

Estimate the fraction.

1.  2.   3.   4.

_____   _____   _____   _____

Activity 6

Add or subtract the fractions by finding the least common multiple.

1. $\frac{5}{8} - \frac{1}{4}$ _____   2. $\frac{3}{10} + \frac{2}{5}$ _____   3. $\frac{5}{6} - \frac{2}{3}$ _____

4. $\frac{4}{5} + \frac{1}{2}$ _____   5. $\frac{5}{6} - \frac{1}{2}$ _____

Name _____ Date _____

Unit Review
Working With Data

Activity 1

The data in the table show the different prices of an airline ticket from Boston to Washington, D.C. Use the data to make a graph that shows the changes in price. Be sure to put labels and a title on your graph.

Date	Price of the Ticket
May 1	$120
May 8	$140
May 15	$150
May 22	$130
May 29	$110

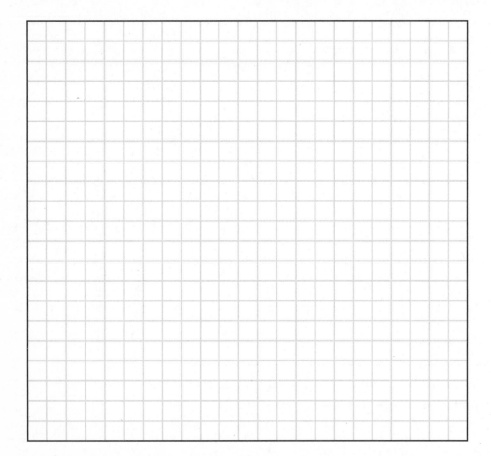

What is the median price of the ticket? _____

Name _____ Date _____

Activity 2

The graph shows how fast different cars went around the race track during a recent stock car race. The speeds are all in seconds. Use the information in the graph to answer questions.

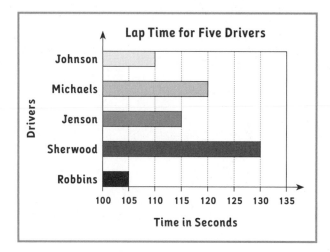

1. How much faster was Jenson than Michaels?

   _____

2. Who was the slowest driver?

   _____

3. What was the time for the fastest driver?

   _____

mBook **Reinforce Understanding**
Use the mBook *Study Guide* to review unit concepts.

Name _____ Date _____

 Skills Maintenance
Multiplication Facts

Activity 1

Solve the multiplication facts.

1. 3 · 7 _____   2. 4 · 8 _____   3. 5 · 6 _____

4. 2 · 9 _____   5. 7 · 7 _____   6. 5 · 7 _____

7. 8 · 7 _____   8. 9 · 9 _____   9. 4 · 4 _____

10. 6 · 3 _____   11. 6 · 9 _____   12. 7 · 5 _____

13. 8 · 8 _____   14. 4 · 3 _____   15. 6 · 2 _____

Name _____ Date _____

%÷ Apply Skills
=× The Concept of Multiplication
<×

Activity 1

Rewrite the whole numbers as fractions with denominators of 1.

Model	$3 \frac{3}{1}$

1. 5 _____   2. 25 _____   3. 79 _____

4. 100 _____   5. 1,599 _____

Activity 2

Tell what the fraction bars represent. Then write the statement as a multiplication problem.

1.

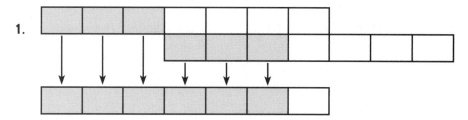

The fraction bars represent _____ sets of _____ .

The multiplication problem is _____ • _____ = _____ .

2.

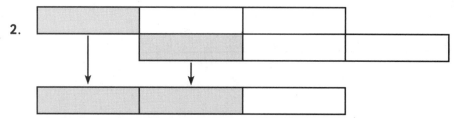

The fraction bars represent _____ sets of _____ .

The multiplication problem is _____ • _____ = _____ .

Name _____ Date _____

 Problem-Solving Activity
Points, Line Segments, Lines, and Rays

On the map, line segments show different sections of the hiking trail. The distances and labels for each section are given in the table. Answer the questions using the map and table.

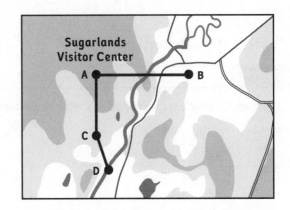

From	To	Label	Distance
Visitor Center	Gatlinburg	A •——• B	$\frac{3}{4}$ mile
Visitor Center	Cove Mountain Point	A •——• C	$\frac{1}{2}$ mile
Cove Mountain Point	Fighting Creek Gap	C •——• D	$\frac{1}{4}$ mile

1. How far is it from the visitor center to Gatlinburg? _____

2. If you were to hike the whole trail, how far would you hike?

    _____

3. If you were to just hike the trail from the visitor center to Fighting Creek Gap, how far would you hike?

    _____

4. How much longer is the trail from the visitor center to Gatlinburg than from the visitor center to Cove Mountain Point?

    _____

mBook Reinforce Understanding
Use the mBook *Study Guide* to review lesson concepts.

Name _____ Date _____

Skills Maintenance
Fractions

Activity 1

Write the whole numbers as fractions.

Model	$2 \quad \frac{2}{1}$

1. 5 _____

2. 17 _____

3. 100 _____

4. 50 _____

5. 27 _____

Rays, Line Segments, Points, and Lines

Activity 2

Write the correct term.

1. A   B   Ray   Line Segment   Point   Line _____

2. D   E   Ray   Line Segment   Point   Line _____

3. X   Y   Ray   Line Segment   Point   Line _____

4. A   Ray   Line Segment   Point   Line _____

5. C   D   Ray   Line Segment   Point   Line _____

Unit 2

Name _____ Date _____

%÷=<x Apply Skills
Finding a Fraction of a Fraction

Activity 1

Solve the multiplication problems. Use the fraction bars to help you.

1. $\frac{2}{6} \cdot \frac{1}{2}$

   Start by drawing the fraction bar for the first number.

   Shade this fraction bar to show $\frac{2}{6}$.

   [ ]

   Then take $\frac{1}{2}$ of the 2 shaded parts, which is _____ part(s).

   What are the total parts? _____   The answer is: _____. $\frac{1}{2} \cdot \frac{2}{6} =$ _____.

2. $\frac{3}{4} \cdot \frac{4}{5}$

   Start by drawing the fraction bar for the second number.

   Shade this fraction bar to show $\frac{4}{5}$.

   [ ]

   Then take $\frac{3}{4}$ of the 4 shaded parts, which is _____ part(s).

   What are the total parts? _____   The answer is: _____. $\frac{3}{4} \cdot \frac{4}{5} =$ _____.

3. $\frac{3}{8} \cdot \frac{2}{3}$

   Start by drawing the fraction bar for the first number.

   Shade this fraction bar to show $\frac{3}{8}$.

   [ ]

   Then take $\frac{2}{3}$ of the 3 shaded parts, which is _____ part(s).

   What are the total parts? _____   The answer is: _____. $\frac{2}{3} \cdot \frac{3}{8} =$ _____.

Name _____ Date _____

 Problem-Solving Activity
Measuring Line Segments

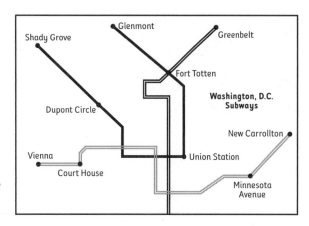

Look at the map of the subway system in Washington, D.C. Then answer the questions measuring in millimeters with a metric ruler.

1. What is the length of the line segment between Shady Grove and Dupont Circle?

_____

2. What is the length of the line segment between Fort Totten and Union Station?

_____

3. Measure and add up the lengths of the line segments between Union Station and Dupont Circle. What is the total length?

_____

4. How much bigger is the line segment from Shady Grove to Dupont Circle than the line segment from the Courthouse to Vienna?

_____

mBook **Reinforce Understanding**
Use the mBook *Study Guide* to review lesson concepts.

Name _____ Date _____

 ## Skills Maintenance
Whole Numbers and Fractions

Activity 1

Rewrite the whole numbers as fractions.

1. 17 _____

2. 29 _____

3. 42 _____

4. 67 _____

5. 125 _____

Name _____ Date _____

 Apply Skills
Multiplying Fractions Using Area Models

Activity 1

Draw area models to find the products of each set of fractions.

1. $\frac{1}{2} \cdot \frac{1}{3}$ _____

2. $\frac{3}{4} \cdot \frac{2}{3}$ _____

3. $\frac{1}{2} \cdot \frac{3}{4}$ _____

4. $\frac{1}{3} \cdot \frac{3}{5}$ _____

Name _____ Date _____

 Problem-Solving Activity
Measuring of Line Segments

Use a metric ruler to answer the questions. Round to the nearest centimeter.

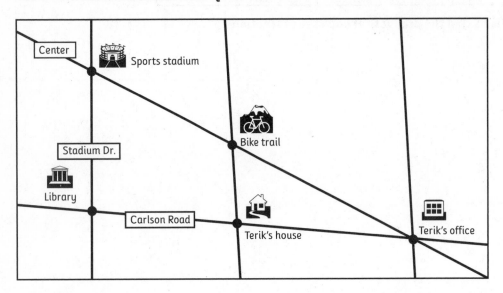

1. Measure the line segment between Terik's house and the library. About how many centimeters long is it?

   _____

2. Measure the line segment between Terik's house and his office building. About how many centimeters long is it?

   _____

3. How much longer is the line segment from Terik's office building to the sports center than it is from Terik's office building to his house?

   _____

4. If Terik travels from his house to his office building, then to the sports stadium, and then to the library, what is the total length of all of those line segments added together? Round each section and add them together.

   _____

mBook **Reinforce Understanding**
Use the mBook *Study Guide* to review lesson concepts.

Name _____ Date _____

Skills Maintenance
Multiplication Facts

Activity 1

Solve the multiplication facts.

1. $3 \cdot 8$ _____

2. $4 \cdot 5$ _____

3. $9 \cdot 7$ _____

4. $8 \cdot 7$ _____

5. $6 \cdot 9$ _____

6. $4 \cdot 4$ _____

7. $10 \cdot 8$ _____

8. $3 \cdot 9$ _____

9. $7 \cdot 6$ _____

Name _____ Date _____

%÷=<x Apply Skills
Multiplying Fractions the Traditional Way

Activity 1

Solve the multiplication problems by multiplying across. You do not need to simplify your answers. Remember that a whole number may be rewritten as a fraction with a denominator of 1.

1. $\dfrac{3}{4} \cdot \dfrac{4}{5}$ _____

2. $\dfrac{5}{7} \cdot \dfrac{1}{2}$ _____

3. $\dfrac{2}{3} \cdot \dfrac{1}{2}$ _____

4. $\dfrac{3}{5} \cdot \dfrac{2}{7}$ _____

5. $\dfrac{2}{9} \cdot \dfrac{3}{4}$ _____

6. $\dfrac{1}{4} \cdot \dfrac{5}{9}$ _____

7. $\dfrac{4}{5} \cdot \dfrac{5}{6}$ _____

8. $\dfrac{6}{8} \cdot \dfrac{2}{3}$ _____

9. $\dfrac{3}{4} \cdot \dfrac{2}{5}$ _____

10. $\dfrac{1}{4} \cdot 5$ _____

11. $\dfrac{2}{10} \cdot \dfrac{3}{4}$ _____

12. $\dfrac{5}{9} \cdot 4$ _____

Name _____ Date _____

Problem-Solving Activity
Angles

Look at the map of the snowmobile trails and landmarks in a park. Write the name of the angle that describes the location of each of the landmarks.

Unit 2

Model	Name the angle that describes the location of the ski resort. ∠IGJ

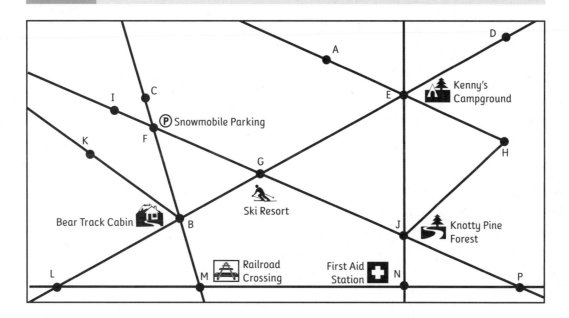

1. Name the angle that describes the location of the snowmobile parking. _____

2. Name the angle that describes the location of the first aid station. _____

3. Name the angle that describes the location of the railroad crossing. _____

4. Name the angle that describes the location of Knotty Pine Forest. _____

5. Name the angle that describes the location of Bear Track Cabin. _____

6. Name the angle that describes the location of Kenny's Campground. _____

mBook Reinforce Understanding
Use the mBook *Study Guide* to review lesson concepts.

Name _____ Date _____

 Skills Maintenance
Multiplication With Fractions

Activity 1

Multiply the fractions and whole numbers by multiplying across. You do not need to simplify your answers.

1. $2 \cdot \frac{1}{3}$ _____

2. $\frac{2}{5} \cdot \frac{5}{8}$ _____

3. $4 \cdot \frac{3}{4}$ _____

4. $\frac{1}{2} \cdot \frac{10}{12}$ _____

5. $\frac{3}{4} \cdot \frac{4}{5}$ _____

6. $\frac{7}{9} \cdot \frac{10}{20}$ _____

7. $6 \cdot \frac{7}{8}$ _____

8. $\frac{8}{9} \cdot \frac{9}{11}$ _____

Angles

Activity 2

Tell the name of each angle.

1.

2.

_____

_____

3.

4.

_____

_____

5.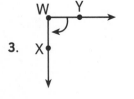

6.

_____

_____

Name _____ Date _____

Apply Skills
Simplifying Fractions

Activity 1

Use the GCF of the numerator and the denominator to simplify the fractions. Write each fraction in simplest form.

1. Simplify the fraction $\frac{3}{9}$. _____

2. Simplify the fraction $\frac{4}{12}$. _____

3. Simplify the fraction $\frac{2}{6}$. _____

4. Simplify the fraction $\frac{8}{12}$. _____

5. Simplify the fraction $\frac{4}{8}$. _____

mBook Reinforce Understanding
Use the mBook *Study Guide* to review lesson concepts.

Name _____ Date _____

Skills Maintenance
Multiplying Fractions the Traditional Way

Activity 1

Solve the problems by multiplying across. You do not need to simplify your answers.

1. $\frac{1}{2} \cdot \frac{3}{4}$ _____

2. $\frac{2}{3} \cdot \frac{1}{4}$ _____

3. $\frac{1}{5} \cdot \frac{2}{1}$ _____

4. $\frac{7}{9} \cdot \frac{1}{5}$ _____

5. $\frac{4}{5} \cdot \frac{5}{6}$ _____

6. $\frac{3}{8} \cdot \frac{1}{4}$ _____

7. $\frac{3}{7} \cdot \frac{2}{3}$ _____

8. $\frac{1}{8} \cdot \frac{3}{1}$ _____

Name _____ Date _____

Problem-Solving Activity
Measuring Angles

Circle the type of angle shown in the picture.

Model		
		(acute) obtuse right

1.   acute   obtuse   right

2.   acute   obtuse   right

3.   acute   obtuse   right

4.   acute   obtuse   right

5.   acute   obtuse   right

6.   acute   obtuse   right

Name _____ Date _____

📝 Problem-Solving Activity
Measuring Angles

Use your wax measuring tool to find the degree measurements of the angles.

1.

_____ degrees

2.

_____ degrees

3.

_____ degrees

4.

_____ degrees

5.

_____ degrees

6.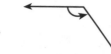

_____ degrees

7.

_____ degrees

8.

_____ degrees

⌨ **mBook** **Reinforce Understanding**
Use the mBook *Study Guide* to review lesson concepts.

62 Unit 2 • Lesson 6

Name _____ Date _____

Skills Maintenance
Multiplication With Fractions

Activity 1

Multiply the fractions by multiplying across. You do not need to simplify your answers.

1. $\dfrac{2}{4} \cdot \dfrac{2}{9}$ _____

2. $\dfrac{3}{8} \cdot \dfrac{5}{9}$ _____

3. $\dfrac{4}{6} \cdot 3$ _____

4. $\dfrac{8}{9} \cdot \dfrac{5}{6}$ _____

Name _____ Date _____

 Apply Skills
Multiplying Factions and Simplifying Answers

Activity 1

Multiply across to find the answer to each problem. Then write the answer in simplest form.

1. $\frac{2}{3} \cdot \frac{1}{4}$ _____

2. $\frac{3}{5} \cdot \frac{5}{9}$ _____

3. $\frac{4}{6} \cdot \frac{3}{4}$ _____

4. $\frac{4}{5} \cdot \frac{5}{6}$ _____

5. $\frac{3}{6} \cdot \frac{2}{5}$ _____

Name _____ Date _____

Problem-Solving Activity
Measuring and Drawing Angles

Use a protractor to draw and measure the angles.

1. Draw an acute angle starting at the dot. Label it XYZ. Measure it.
    What is its measurement?

    _____

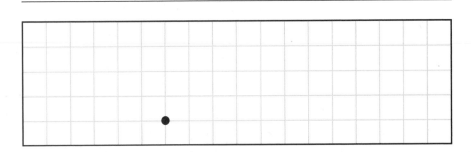

2. Draw an obtuse angle starting at the dot. Label it LMN. Measure it.
    What is its measurement?

    _____

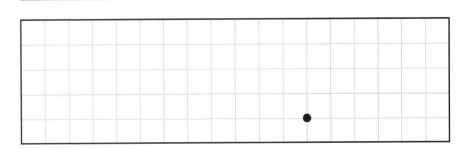

3. Draw a 65 degree angle starting at the dot. Label it ABC. What type
    of angle is it?

    _____

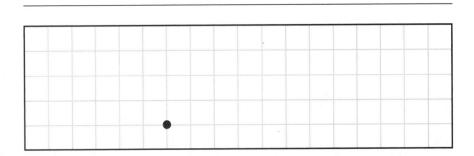

Name _____ Date _____

4. Draw a right angle starting at the dot. Measure it. What is its measurement?

_____

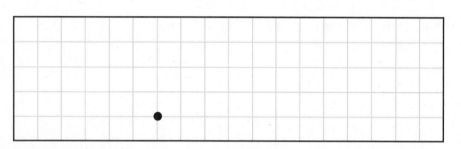

5. Draw an acute angle starting at the dot. Measure it. What is its measurement?

_____

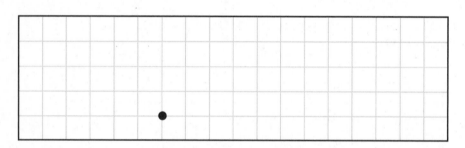

6. Draw an angle that is 10 degrees more than the angle you drew in Problem 5. What is its measurement?

_____

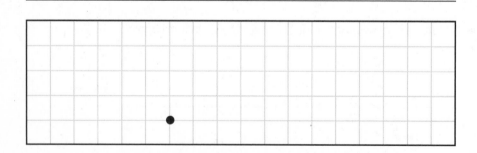

mBook Reinforce Understanding
Use the mBook *Study Guide* to review lesson concepts.

Name _____ Date _____

Skills Maintenance
Dividing With Whole Numbers

Activity 1

Divide the whole numbers using any method.

1. $8\overline{)56}$

2. $9\overline{)87}$

3. $7\overline{)45}$

4. $6\overline{)50}$

Name _____ Date _____

%÷ Apply Skills
Dividing Fractions

Activity 1

Use the fraction bars to help you solve these division problems.

1. $2 \div \frac{1}{4}$ _____ ⌐These units are fourths. How many are in 2?

1				2			

2. $5 \div \frac{1}{2}$ _____ ⌐These units are halves. How many are in 5?

1	2	3	4	5

3. $6 \div \frac{2}{3}$ _____ ⌐These units are thirds. How many $\frac{2}{3}$* are in 6?

1	2	3	4	5	6

Note: The units are thirds, but you want to look at units of $\frac{2}{3}$.
Be sure to count sections of $\frac{2}{3}$ and not $\frac{1}{3}$.

Activity 2

Use the traditional method of invert and multiply to solve the division problems. Simplify the quotients.

1. $\frac{2}{1} \div \frac{1}{3}$ _____ 2. $\frac{3}{5} \div \frac{5}{8}$ _____ 3. $\frac{4}{4} \div \frac{3}{4}$ _____

4. $\frac{1}{2} \div \frac{3}{8}$ _____ 5. $\frac{6}{1} \div \frac{1}{2}$ _____ 6. $\frac{3}{8} \div \frac{5}{9}$ _____

7. $\frac{4}{12} \div \frac{3}{16} =$ _____ 8. $\frac{11}{12} \div \frac{7}{8} =$ _____

Name _____ Date _____

Problem-Solving Activity
Using Measurement Tools With a Map

We will design a city on a map using a protractor and ruler. Place certain landmarks on the map. Draw the picture of the landmark or write the words that describe the landmark, or both. Make the measurement and record it in the table.

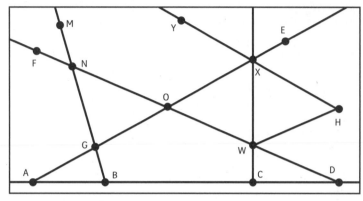

1. Place the courthouse 🏛 at the vertex of ∠BCW. Measure the angle and record its measurement in the table.

2. Place the park 🌲 on line segment BC. Measure the line segment in cm. and record the measurement in the table.

3. Place Quiet Lane Townhouses 🏠🏠🏠 on line segment AG. Measure the line segment in centimeters and record the measurement in the table.

4. Place the stadium 🏟 at the vertex of ∠MNO. Measure the angle and record its measurement in the table.

Landmark Name	Picture	Location	Measurement
Courthouse	🏛	∠BCW	
Park	🌲	Line segment BC	
Quiet Lane Townhouses	🏠🏠🏠	Line Segment AG	
Stadium	🏟	∠MNO	

mBook Reinforce Understanding
Use the mBook *Study Guide* to review lesson concepts.

Name _____ Date _____

 ## Skills Maintenance
Multiplying and Simplifying

Activity 1

Multiply the fractions, and simplify the answers.

1. $\frac{1}{3} \cdot \frac{4}{2}$ _____

2. $\frac{4}{6} \cdot \frac{5}{4}$ _____

3. $\frac{4}{3} \cdot \frac{3}{6}$ _____

4. $\frac{2}{5} \cdot \frac{5}{6}$ _____

5. $\frac{1}{3} \cdot \frac{2}{5}$ _____

Name _____ Date _____

Apply Skills
Dividing Fractions by Fractions

Activity 1

Divide the fractions using the fraction bars.

1. $\frac{3}{4} \div \frac{1}{4}$

The parts in the top bar are fourths. How many of these parts are in $\frac{3}{4}$? _____

2. $\frac{5}{6} \div \frac{1}{6}$

The parts in the top bar are sixths. How many of these parts are in $\frac{5}{6}$? _____

3. $\frac{1}{2} \div \frac{1}{4}$

The parts in the top bar are fourths. How many of these parts are in $\frac{1}{2}$? _____

4. $\frac{3}{4} \div \frac{1}{8}$

The parts in the top bar are eighths. How many of these parts are in $\frac{3}{4}$? _____

5. $\frac{1}{2} \div \frac{1}{16}$

The parts in the top bar are sixteenths. How many of these parts are in $\frac{1}{2}$? _____

Name _____ Date _____

Problem-Solving Activity
Measuring Angle of Ramps on a Motorbike Race Course

Your company has been contracted to design a race course for motorbike racing. You are in charge of mapping out the course and designing the ramps the bikes will use for jumping. Measure the angles of the ramps like this:

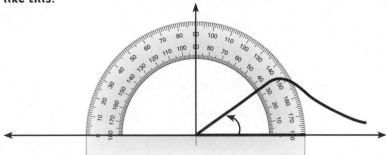

It's important that you measure the angles very carefully. There are regulations and restrictions for the angles of the ramps. One of the rules is that no jump can be steeper than 35 degrees.

On the motorbike race course layout you have been given, notice that there are six ramps. Your job is to measure the angle of each of the ramps and tell how many degrees the angle is. Circle any of the ramps that are too steep (based on the rule that no jump can be steeper than 35 degrees.)

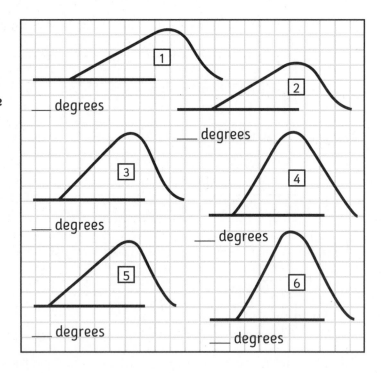

mBook Reinforce Understanding
Use the mBook *Study Guide* to review lesson concepts.

Name _____ Date _____

Skills Maintenance
Multiplying and Simplifying

Activity 1

Multiply the fractions and simplify.

1. $\frac{6}{8} \cdot \frac{3}{4}$ _____

2. $\frac{3}{5} \cdot \frac{1}{3}$ _____

3. $\frac{2}{6} \cdot \frac{9}{3}$ _____

Angles

Activity 2

Identify the name and type of angle (acute, obtuse, or right).

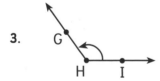

1. Angle _____ is _____ .

2. Angle _____ is _____ .

3. Angle _____ is _____ .

Name _____ Date _____

 Apply Skills
The Traditional Method for Dividing Fractions

Activity 1

Divide the fractions using the traditional method. Write the quotient in its simplest form.

1. $\dfrac{2}{3} \div \dfrac{1}{8}$ _____

2. $\dfrac{1}{4} \div \dfrac{2}{8}$ _____

3. $\dfrac{5}{6} \div \dfrac{3}{4}$ _____

4. $\dfrac{3}{100} \div \dfrac{1}{4}$ _____

5. $\dfrac{3}{25} \div \dfrac{6}{7}$ _____

6. $\dfrac{6}{16} \div \dfrac{5}{6}$ _____

mBook Reinforce Understanding
Use the mBook *Study Guide* to review lesson concepts.

Name _____ Date _____

 Skills Maintenance
Simplifying Fractions

Activity 1

Multiply the fractions. Then simplify the answer.

1. $\frac{3}{9} \cdot \frac{2}{3}$ _____

2. $\frac{4}{8} \cdot \frac{4}{6}$ _____

3. $\frac{6}{9} \cdot \frac{3}{6}$ _____

Activity 2

Divide the fractions using invert and multiply. Then simplify the answer using the GCF. Write the answer in simplest form.

1. $\frac{1}{2} \div \frac{1}{8}$ _____

2. $\frac{3}{4} \div \frac{5}{6}$ _____

3. $\frac{4}{6} \div \frac{5}{4}$ _____

Name _____ Date _____

Problem-Solving Activity
Measuring With a U.S. Customary Ruler

Measure each of the line segments using a metric ruler, and round to the nearest millimeter. Then use a U.S. customary ruler, and round to the nearest $\frac{1}{4}$ inch.

1. Measure line segment AB.

   A •———————————————————————————• B

   AB is _____ mm.

   AB is _____ in.

2. Measure line segment CD.

   C •———————————• D

   CD is _____ mm.

   CD is _____ in.

3. Measure line segment EF.

   E •———————• F

   EF is _____ mm.

   EF is _____ in.

4. Measure line segment GH.

   G •———————————————————• H

   GH is _____ mm.

   GH is _____ in.

mBook Reinforce Understanding
Use the mBook *Study Guide* to review lesson concepts.

Name _____ Date _____

Skills Maintenance
Multiply, Divide, and Simplify Fractions

Activity 1

Use traditional algorithms to multiply and divide the fractions. Simplify the answers.

1. $\frac{3}{4} \cdot \frac{2}{9}$ _____

2. $\frac{4}{5} \div \frac{3}{4}$ _____

3. $\frac{7}{8} \cdot \frac{4}{6}$ _____

4. $\frac{3}{8} \div \frac{6}{2}$ _____

Name _____ Date _____

%÷ Apply Skills
Multiplying Three Fractions and Simplifying Using the GCF

Activity 1

Solve the multiplication problems with three fractions. Simplify the answer.

1. $\frac{4}{5} \cdot \frac{1}{3} \cdot \frac{1}{2}$ _____

2. $\frac{1}{8} \cdot \frac{1}{2} \cdot \frac{1}{5}$ _____

3. $\frac{3}{5} \cdot \frac{3}{4} \cdot \frac{1}{5}$ _____

4. $\frac{1}{3} \cdot \frac{24}{25} \cdot \frac{1}{4}$ _____

Name _____ Date _____

 ## Problem-Solving Activity
Introduction to the Compass

Draw a house using a compass and a protractor. The walls must meet the floor at exactly 90-degree angles, or the house will collapse. Make the top angle in the roof 90 degrees as well. Use the compass to draw overlapping circles to help you measure exact angles.

mBook Reinforce Understanding
Use the mBook *Study Guide* to review lesson concepts.

Name _____ Date _____

 Skills Maintenance
Multiplying Three Fractions and Simplifying the Answer

Activity 1

Multiply the fractions. Simplify your answer.

1. $\frac{1}{3} \cdot \frac{2}{5} \cdot \frac{4}{2}$ _____

2. $\frac{2}{4} \cdot \frac{3}{6} \cdot \frac{5}{8}$ _____

3. $\frac{4}{6} \cdot \frac{3}{2} \cdot \frac{2}{3}$ _____

Name _____ Date _____

Apply Skills
Comparing Multiplication and Division of Fractions

Activity 1

In each problem there is an error. Find the error and tell what it is. Explain how you know it is wrong. Then fix the error and solve the problem correctly.

1. $\frac{3}{5} \cdot \frac{1}{3}$ INCORRECT: $\frac{3}{5} \cdot \frac{3}{1} = \frac{3 \cdot 3}{5 \cdot 1} = \frac{9}{5}$

   What is the error?

   _____

   _____

   How do you know it's wrong?

   _____

   _____

   Fix the error and solve the problem the correct way.

   _____

2. $\frac{3}{4} \div \frac{1}{2} = ?$ INCORRECT: $\frac{3}{4} \div \frac{1}{2} = \frac{3 \cdot 1}{4 \cdot 2} = \frac{3}{8}$

   What is the error?

   _____

   _____

   How do you know it's wrong?

   _____

   _____

   Fix the error and solve the problem the correct way.

   _____

Name _____ Date _____

Problem-Solving Activity
Working With a Compass

A solar eclipse occurs when the moon passes between the Earth and the Sun. This causes the sun to seem to disappear in the middle of the day. This phenomenon used to frighten people, but astronomers know now that there is a mathematical explanation.

Bisect the angle that is formed between the Moon and the Sun. Find the measurement of the two new angles.

_____

_____

_____

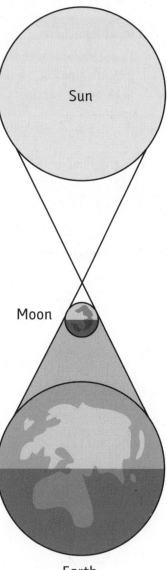

Sun

Moon

Earth

mBook Reinforce Understanding
Use the mBook *Study Guide* to review lesson concepts.

Name _____ Date _____

 ## Skills Maintenance
Fractions

Activity 1

Multiply, divide, and simplify the fractions.

1. $\frac{2}{3} \cdot \frac{3}{5} \cdot \frac{1}{2}$ _____

2. $\frac{3}{9} \cdot \frac{4}{8}$ _____

3. $\frac{8}{12} \div \frac{1}{4}$ _____

4. $\frac{3}{9} \div \frac{1}{3}$ _____

Name _____ Date _____

 Apply Skills
Common Fraction Errors: Keeping It All Straight

Activity 1

Find the error in each of the problems. Describe the error, then solve the
problem correctly.

1. $\frac{1}{5} + \frac{17}{25} = \frac{18}{30}$

_____

_____

_____

_____

2. $\frac{6}{3} \cdot \frac{2}{4} = \frac{24}{12} \cdot \frac{6}{12} = \frac{144}{144}$

_____

_____

_____

_____

3. $\frac{1}{3} \div \frac{1}{6} = \frac{2}{6} \div \frac{1}{6} = \frac{2}{6}$

_____

_____

_____

_____

4. $\frac{6}{10} - \frac{1}{3} = \frac{5}{7}$

_____

_____

_____

_____

Name _____ Date _____

 ### Problem-Solving Activity
Drawing Triangles With a Compass

Use your compass and a ruler to make an equilateral triangle that has sides 4 inches long. Draw arcs to make the triangle. Then draw a second triangle. Make two circles to make an equilateral triangle that is 33 millimeters on each side.

_____

_____

mBook Reinforce Understanding
Use the mBook *Study Guide* to review lesson concepts.

Name _____ Date _____

Skills Maintenance
Identifying Angles

Activity 1

Give the name of the angles using the letters given and the angle symbol (remember, it looks like this: ∠). Tell what type of angle it is (right, obtuse, acute).

1.

This angle is called: _____

What type of angle is it? (circle one)   right   obtuse   acute

2.

This angle is called: _____

What type of angle is it? (circle one)   right   obtuse   acute

3.

This angle is called: _____

What type of angle is it? (circle one)   right   obtuse   acute

4.

This angle is called: _____

What type of angle is it? (circle one)   right   obtuse   acute

Name _____ Date _____

Unit Review
Multiplication and Division of Fractions

Activity 1

Solve the division problems. Simplify your answers.

1. $\frac{2}{6} \div \frac{4}{3}$ _____

2. $\frac{3}{8} \div \frac{1}{8}$ _____

3. $\frac{4}{5} \div \frac{1}{5}$ _____

4. $\frac{3}{9} \div \frac{2}{3}$ _____

5. $\frac{4}{6} \div \frac{1}{3}$ _____

6. $\frac{5}{6} \div \frac{2}{12}$ _____

Activity 2

Multiply the fractions. Simplify your answers.

1. $\frac{2}{6} \cdot \frac{3}{7}$ _____

2. $\frac{3}{8} \cdot \frac{2}{3}$ _____

3. $\frac{5}{9} \cdot \frac{1}{5}$ _____

4. $\frac{3}{9} \cdot \frac{2}{4}$ _____

5. $\frac{4}{6} \cdot \frac{3}{4}$ _____

6. $\frac{1}{6} \cdot \frac{3}{5}$ _____

Activity 3

Solve a mix of operations with fractions. Remember the rules for each algorithm. Simplify the answers.

1. $\frac{3}{5} + \frac{2}{4}$ _____

2. $\frac{8}{9} \div \frac{2}{3}$ _____

3. $\frac{3}{9} \cdot \frac{2}{4}$ _____

4. $\frac{1}{3} - \frac{1}{9}$ _____

5. $\frac{7}{9} - \frac{1}{3}$ _____

6. $\frac{3}{5} \div \frac{4}{2}$ _____

7. $\frac{3}{4} + \frac{4}{5}$ _____

8. $\frac{8}{9} \cdot \frac{2}{3}$ _____

Name _____ Date _____

Unit Review
Tools for Measurement and Construction

Activity 1

Measure the line segments using both millimeters and inches. Round to the nearest whole unit.

1. _____

   Millimeters _____   Inches _____

2. _____

   Millimeters _____   Inches _____

3. _____

   Millimeters _____   Inches _____

4. _____

   Millimeters _____   Inches _____

Activity 2

Use a protractor to tell the measure of each angle. Then name the type of angle (obtuse, acute, or right).

1.

_____

2.

_____

3.

_____

4.

_____

5.

_____

Name _____ Date _____

Activity 3

Use a protractor to make the angles.

1. Make a 50° angle.

2. Make a 72° angle.

3. Make a 12° angle.

mBook Reinforce Understanding
Use the mBook *Study Guide* to review unit concepts.

Name _____ Date _____

 Skills Maintenance
Fractions That are Greater Than or Equal to 1

Activity 1

Circle the fractions that are greater than or equal to 1.

$\frac{5}{4}$ $\frac{3}{9}$ $\frac{8}{7}$ $\frac{1}{3}$ $\frac{9}{1}$

$\frac{7}{8}$ $\frac{6}{9}$ $\frac{8}{4}$ $\frac{2}{4}$ $\frac{11}{12}$

$\frac{1}{2}$ $\frac{5}{1}$ $\frac{7}{1}$ $\frac{4}{4}$ $\frac{3}{2}$

Name _____ Date _____

%÷ Apply Skills
Improper Fractions and Mixed Numbers

Activity 1

Change the improper fractions to mixed numbers.

1. $\frac{11}{4}$ _____

2. $\frac{9}{8}$ _____

3. $\frac{11}{6}$ _____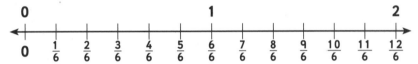

Activity 2

Show the improper fractions by shading the fraction bars or shapes. Then write the mixed numbers.

1. $\frac{3}{2}$ _____

2. $\frac{7}{3}$ _____

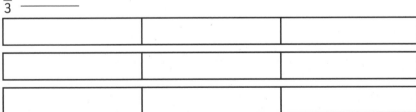

3. $\frac{18}{4}$ _____

Name _____ Date _____

 Problem-Solving Activity
Working With Shapes

Draw two objects on the grid. For each object, show what it would look like when you:

1. Slide it

2. Flip it

3. Turn it

mBook **Reinforce Understanding**
Use the mBook *Study Guide* to review lesson concepts.

Name _____ Date _____

Skills Maintenance
Improper Fractions

Activity 1

Change the improper fractions into mixed numbers. Use the number line, fraction bars, and circles to help you.

1. $\frac{13}{4}$ _____

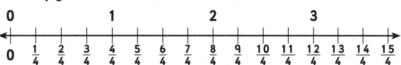

2. $\frac{16}{5}$ _____

3. $\frac{22}{4}$ _____

Transformations

Activity 2

Identify the transformation that is taking place between each pair of shapes. Circle the correct answer.

1.   Slide   or   Flip

2.   Slide   or   Flip

3.   Slide   or   Flip

4.   Slide   or   Flip

5.   Slide   or   Flip

Unit 3

Name _____ Date _____

 Apply Skills
Adding and Subtracting Mixed Numbers: The LAPS Process

Activity 1

Shade the first number, then use Xs to subtract the second number.

1. $3\frac{3}{4}$

    $-1\frac{1}{4}$

Activity 2

Use LAPS to solve the mixed number problems. Complete each step in the boxes.

1. $3\frac{1}{6} + 5\frac{4}{6}$ _____

L	
A	
P	
S	

2. $9\frac{3}{5} - 4\frac{1}{5}$ _____

L	
A	
P	
S	

Name _____ Date _____

Problem-Solving Activity
Solving Word Problems With Mixed Numbers

Before the Scatter Plots can move things to the second floor of the house, they need to fix the staircase. This will require accurate measurement. Help the Scatter Plots by solving the four problems.

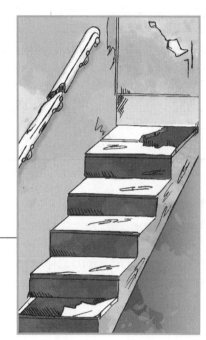

1. The step at the bottom of the staircase is broken. The Scatter Plots have a board $4\frac{5}{8}$ feet long. The board only nee to be $3\frac{3}{8}$ feet long. How much of the board needs to be cut off?

    _____

2. There is a hole in the floor at the top of the staircase. Two boards are needed to cover the hole. Each board is $1\frac{1}{3}$ feet wide. How wide is the hole in the floor?

    _____

3. Another part of the floor needs to be replaced. It can be done with two boards. The first board is $3\frac{5}{16}$ feet long and the second board is $4\frac{9}{16}$ feet long. How long is the part of the floor that needs to be replaced?

    _____

4. One railing on the staircase is cracked. The only board the band members have to fix the problem is $5\frac{7}{8}$ feet long. The new railing should be $5\frac{1}{8}$ feet long. How much will have to be cut off to make the board fit?

    _____

mBook **Reinforce Understanding**
Use the mBook *Study Guide* to review lesson concepts.

Name _____ Date _____

 Skills Maintenance
Improper Fractions

Activity 1

Change the improper fractions into mixed numbers. Use number lines or fraction bars to help you, if necessary.

1. $\frac{5}{4}$ _____

2. $\frac{19}{2}$ _____

3. $\frac{7}{5}$ _____

4. $\frac{25}{8}$ _____

5. $\frac{4}{3}$ _____

6. $\frac{13}{6}$ _____

Transformations

Activity 2

Identify the transformation that is taking place between each pair of shapes. Circle the correct answer.

1. Slide or Flip or Both

2. Slide or Flip or Both

3. Slide or Flip or Both

4. Slide or Flip or Both

5. Slide or Flip or Both

6. Slide or Flip or Both

7. Slide or Flip or Both

8. Slide or Flip or Both

Name _____ Date _____

 Apply Skills
Adding and Subtracting Mixed Numbers With Unlike Denominators

Activity 1

Use the LAPS method to solve the mixed number problems. Complete each step in the boxes labeled L-A-P-S. Be sure to find a common denominator in the A—alter step if the fractions have different denominators.

1. $2\frac{3}{4} - 1\frac{1}{2}$ _____

L	
A	
P	
S	

2. $1\frac{1}{4} + 3\frac{2}{4}$ _____

L	
A	
P	
S	

Name _____ Date _____

✎ Problem-Solving Activity
More Word Problems With Mixed Numbers

Now the Scatter Plots have to replace the pipe in the bathroom and fix the hole in the wall. Help the band by solving the problems.

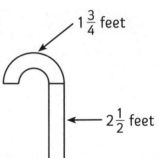

1. The pipe that goes up the inside of the wall bends in two places. The first part is $2\frac{1}{2}$ feet long. After it bends, it is $1\frac{3}{4}$ feet long. How long is the entire pipe?

    _____

2. The next segment of pipe goes under the floor. An arrow points to the section of the pipe that needs to be replaced. It is $5\frac{1}{8}$ feet long. The band has a pipe that is $5\frac{3}{4}$ feet. How much will they have to cut off?

    _____

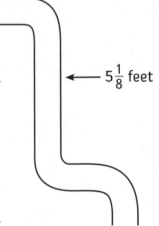

3. Now the Scatter Plots need to put up drywall. The drywall has to be cut wide enough for the space in the wall. The space is $3\frac{3}{8}$ feet wide and the band has a piece of drywall that is $3\frac{3}{4}$ feet wide. How much has to be cut off to make the drywall fit?

    _____

4. The next step in fixing the wall is to put tape on the wall where the boards connect. This will make it so that the lines in the wall don't show when the room is painted. The tape comes in large rolls. Two strips of tape are needed. The first strip is $7\frac{1}{2}$ feet long and the second is $6\frac{3}{8}$ feet long. How much tape do they need for the wall?

    _____

mBook Reinforce Understanding
Use the mBook *Study Guide* to review lesson concepts.

Name _____ Date _____

 ### Skills Maintenance
Improper Fractions, Mixed Numbers

Activity 1

Convert the improper fractions to mixed numbers.

1. $\dfrac{11}{9}$ _____

2. $\dfrac{12}{5}$ _____

3. $\dfrac{25}{8}$ _____

4. $\dfrac{74}{9}$ _____

Activity 2

Solve the mixed number addition and subtraction problems with like and unlike denominators. Use LAPS to help you. Show all the steps.

1. $4\dfrac{2}{3} - 3\dfrac{1}{2}$ _____

_____

_____

_____

_____

2. $7\dfrac{1}{5} + 8\dfrac{1}{4}$ _____

_____

_____

_____

_____

3. $17\dfrac{2}{3} - 9\dfrac{1}{3}$ _____

_____

_____

_____

_____

Name _____ Date _____

Problem-Solving Activity

Patterns in Tessellations: What Is in the Mind's Eye?

Measure each highlighted angle using your protractor.

1. Measure the angle. It is _____.

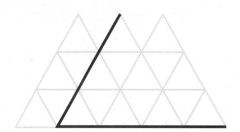

2. Measure the angle. It is _____.

3. Measure the angle. It is _____.

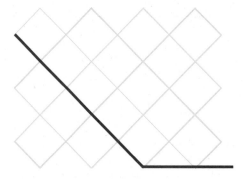

4. Measure the angle. It is _____.

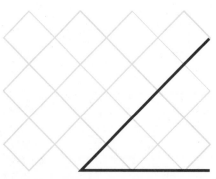

mBook Reinforce Understanding

Use the mBook *Study Guide* to review lesson concepts.

Name _____ Date _____

 Skills Maintenance
Mracted **Mixed Numbers**

Activity 1

Add or subtract the mixed numbers with like and unlike denominators.
Use the LAPS strategy.

1. $1\frac{1}{2} + 2\frac{1}{4}$ _____

_____

_____

_____

_____

2. $3\frac{7}{8} - 2\frac{2}{8}$ _____

_____

_____

_____

_____

3. $5\frac{1}{3} + 6\frac{1}{2}$ _____

_____

_____

_____

_____

4. $12\frac{5}{6} - 6\frac{1}{2}$ _____

_____

_____

_____

_____

Name _____ Date _____

%÷ Apply Skills
<≥×
Regrouping With Mixed Numbers

Activity 1

Solve the problems using LAPS.

1. $6\frac{3}{4} + 7\frac{3}{4}$ _____

L	
A	
P	
S	

2. $9\frac{1}{8} - 2\frac{3}{8}$ _____

L	
A	
P	
S	

3. $5\frac{2}{6} - 1\frac{5}{6}$ _____

L	
A	
P	
S	

Name _____ Date _____

Skills Maintenance
Mixed Numbers

Activity 1

Solve. Regroup if necessary.

1. $3\frac{4}{5} - 2\frac{1}{10}$ _____

2. $6\frac{5}{9} + 5\frac{2}{3}$ _____

3. $18\frac{1}{8} - 9\frac{5}{8}$ _____

4. $14\frac{3}{7} - 13\frac{5}{7}$ _____

Name _____ Date _____

Apply Skills
Remember to Simplify

| Activity 1 |

Use LAPS to solve the problems. Be sure the answer is in its simplest form.

1. $5\frac{3}{4} + 2\frac{9}{12}$ _____

_____

_____

_____

_____

2. $6\frac{7}{9} - 2\frac{1}{9}$ _____

_____

_____

_____

3. $5\frac{8}{9} + 3\frac{7}{9}$ _____

_____

_____

_____

4. $4\frac{7}{10} - 1\frac{1}{5}$ _____

_____

_____

_____

_____

Name _____ Date _____

Problem-Solving Activity
Measurement and Tessellations

You learned to draw tessellations using a template. Now you have the chance to make one with a ruler and scissors. Start by drawing a shape that will be used in the tessellation.

Step 1
Use thick paper or part of a manila folder to draw a right angle. You will need to use the side of the ruler to make sure that you have a right angle.

Step 2
Mark off the horizontal line so that it is $2\frac{1}{2}$ inches. Also, draw the vertical side of your angle so that it measures $2\frac{3}{4}$ inches.

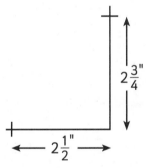

Step 3
Connect the points on the side so that you have a triangle.

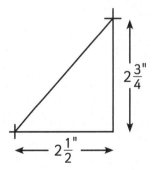

Name _____ Date _____

Step 4

Now you want to reflect this triangle and make another one. Just make the vertical line longer so that it measures $2\frac{3}{4}$ inches below the line.

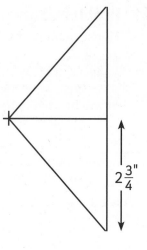

Step 5

Put a notch in the triangles. Measure in $\frac{1}{2}$ inches from the right angle and make a mark. Then connect this point to the two angles, as shown.

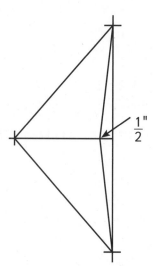

Step 6

Cut it out. It should look like this shape. You will use this template to make a tessellation in the next lesson.

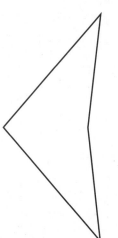

mBook Reinforce Understanding
Use the mBook *Study Guide* to review lesson concepts.

Name _____ Date _____

Skills Maintenance
Adding Fractions

Activity 1

Add the fractions. Convert the answer to a mixed number.

1. $\frac{2}{2} + \frac{2}{2} + \frac{2}{2} + \frac{1}{2}$

    _____

2. $\frac{3}{3} + \frac{3}{3} + \frac{3}{3} + \frac{3}{3} + \frac{3}{3} + \frac{2}{3}$

    _____

3. $\frac{7}{7} + \frac{7}{7} + \frac{5}{7}$

    _____

4. $\frac{8}{8} + \frac{8}{8} + \frac{8}{8} + \frac{3}{8}$

    _____

5. $\frac{4}{4} + \frac{4}{4} + \frac{4}{4} + \frac{4}{4} + \frac{4}{4} + \frac{4}{4} + \frac{4}{4} + \frac{3}{4}$

    _____

6. $\frac{9}{9} + \frac{9}{9} + \frac{9}{9} + \frac{9}{9} + \frac{7}{9}$

    _____

7. $\frac{10}{10} + \frac{9}{10}$

    _____

Name _____ Date _____

%÷ Apply Skills
=<x Converting Mixed Numbers Into Improper Fractions

Activity 1

Convert the mixed numbers into improper fractions.

1. Change $9\frac{2}{5}$ into an improper fraction. _____

2. Change $7\frac{3}{4}$ into an improper fraction. _____

3. Change $8\frac{5}{9}$ into an improper fraction. _____

4. Change $3\frac{7}{8}$ into an improper fraction. _____

Name _____ Date _____

 ## Problem-Solving Activity
Creating a Tessellation

On a blank sheet of paper, use the shape you made in the last lesson to construct your own tessellation. When you have finished, look for the lines in your mind's eye that help create the tessellation pattern. If you have time, draw the lines using a straightedge. Use a protractor to measure the angles.

Unit 3

mBook Reinforce Understanding
Use the mBook *Study Guide* to review lesson concepts.

Name _____ Date _____

Skills Maintenance
Converting Fractions

Activity 1

Convert the mixed numbers into improper fractions and vice versa.

1. $3\frac{2}{3}$ _____

2. $4\frac{1}{2}$ _____

3. $2\frac{3}{8}$ _____

4. $\frac{11}{4}$ _____

5. $\frac{7}{3}$ _____

6. $\frac{11}{2}$ _____

Transformations

Activity 2

Identify the transformation that is taking place between each pair of shapes. Circle the correct answer.

1. slide   or   reflection

2. slide   or   reflection

3. slide   or   reflection

4. slide   or   reflection

5. slide   or   reflection

6. slide   or   reflection

Name _____ Date _____

 Apply Skills
Multiplying Mixed Numbers

Activity 1

Multiply the mixed numbers using LAPS. Change all the mixed numbers into improper fractions in the A—alter step. Then multiply. In the S—simplify step, change the fraction back into a mixed number.

1. $3\frac{1}{3} \cdot 2\frac{1}{4}$ _____

_____

_____

_____

2. $1\frac{1}{8} \cdot 5\frac{1}{2}$ _____

_____

_____

_____

3. $1\frac{1}{3} \cdot 3\frac{2}{3}$ _____

_____

_____

_____

4. $2\frac{1}{2} \cdot 1\frac{1}{5}$ _____

_____

_____

_____

Name _____ Date _____

Problem-Solving Activity
Floor Plans

Look at the floor plan for Todd's summer cabin. Todd wants to carpet the entire lower floor except for the porch. Use the dimensions given for each room to compute how much carpet will be needed. Remember, to find the area of a rectangle you multiply length · width.

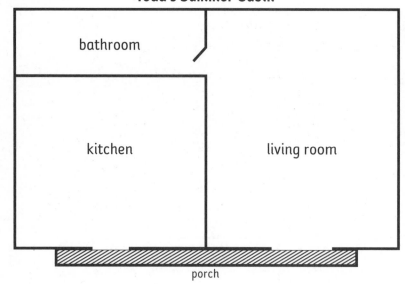

Todd's Summer Cabin

bathroom

kitchen

living room

porch

Bathroom Dimensions

$2\frac{1}{3}$ yards × $4\frac{1}{2}$ yards

Kitchen Dimensions

$8\frac{2}{3}$ yards × $4\frac{1}{2}$ yards

Living Room Dimensions

11 yards × $4\frac{1}{2}$ yards

Porch Dimensions

1 yard × 11 yards

Carpet needed:

Bathroom _____

Kitchen _____

Living Room _____

Total _____

mBook Reinforce Understanding
Use the mBook *Study Guide* to review lesson concepts.

Name _____ Date _____

Skills Maintenance
Multiplying Mixed Numbers

Activity 1

Multiply the mixed numbers. Simplify your answer.

1. $1\frac{2}{3} \cdot 2\frac{1}{2}$ _____

2. $3\frac{1}{5} \cdot 4\frac{2}{7}$ _____

3. $4\frac{1}{2} \cdot 7\frac{1}{4}$ _____

4. $2\frac{1}{4} \cdot 3\frac{4}{5}$ _____

5. $1\frac{2}{8} \cdot 2\frac{2}{3}$ _____

6. $2\frac{5}{9} \cdot 1\frac{1}{6}$ _____

Name _____ Date _____

Problem-Solving Activity
Measuring the Angle of Rotation

One or more transformations is occurring between each pair of shapes. Identify the transformation(s): reflection (flip), translation (slide), and/or rotation (turn). For some questions, you might need to circle more than one type of transformation.

1.

Reflection   Translation   Rotation

2.

Reflection   Translation   Rotation

3.

Reflection   Translation   Rotation

4.

Reflection   Translation   Rotation

5.

Reflection   Translation   Rotation

6.

Reflection   Translation   Rotation

7.

Reflection   Translation   Rotation

8.

Reflection   Translation   Rotation

Name _____ Date _____

Problem-Solving Activity
Measuring the Angle of Rotation

Rotate the shapes using a ruler and a protractor. As you rotate each shape, think about the different occasions where the shape looks like it could have been created by a rotation or a reflection, for instance at 0 degrees and at 180 degrees. Also, think about why the rotated shapes cannot be mistaken for translations.

1. 135 degrees

2. 45 degrees

3. 90 degrees

4. 25 degrees

mBook Reinforce Understanding
Use the mBook *Study Guide* to review lesson concepts.

Name _____ Date _____

Skills Maintenance
Fractions

Activity 1

Convert the mixed numbers to improper fractions and improper fractions to mixed numbers.

1. $5\frac{3}{4}$ _____

2. $\frac{11}{4}$ _____

3. $\frac{26}{9}$ _____

4. $7\frac{2}{3}$ _____

5. $\frac{73}{8}$ _____

6. $8\frac{1}{9}$ _____

7. $10\frac{2}{3}$ _____

8. $\frac{34}{8}$ _____

Transformations

Activity 2

One or more transformations is occurring between each pair of shapes. Identify the transformation(s): reflection (flip), translation (slide), and/or rotation (turn). For some questions, you might need to circle more than one type of transformation.

1.

Reflection   Translation   Rotation

2.

Reflection   Translation   Rotation

3.

Reflection   Translation   Rotation

4.

Reflection   Translation   Rotation

5.

Reflection   Translation   Rotation

Name _____ Date _____

%÷ Apply Skills
Dividing Mixed Numbers

Activity 1

Use LAPS to divide the mixed numbers. Remember to change the mixed numbers to improper fractions in the A—alter step. Also, remember to flip the second number in the P—perform step. Then, in the last step, remember to change the answer back to a mixed number.

1. $3\frac{1}{2} \div 1\frac{1}{9}$ _____

_____

_____

_____

_____

2. $2\frac{1}{3} \div 1\frac{1}{4}$ _____

_____

_____

_____

_____

3. $3\frac{1}{3} \div 2\frac{2}{5}$ _____

_____

_____

_____

_____

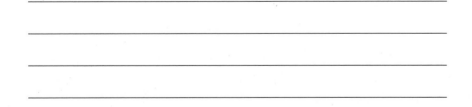

mBook Reinforce Understanding
Use the mBook *Study Guide* to review lesson concepts.

Unit 3

Name _____ Date _____

Skills Maintenance
Dividing Fractions

Activity 1

Divide the fractions. Remember to flip the second number and multiply.
You do not need to simplify your answers.

1. $\frac{5}{4} \div \frac{3}{2}$

_____

2. $\frac{7}{6} \div \frac{4}{3}$

_____

3. $\frac{8}{2} \div \frac{7}{6}$

_____

4. $\frac{9}{3} \div \frac{5}{3}$

_____

5. $\frac{3}{2} \div \frac{7}{9}$

_____

6. $\frac{9}{8} \div \frac{9}{3}$

_____

7. $\frac{4}{3} \div \frac{3}{4}$

_____

Name _____ Date _____

Apply Skills
Keeping It All Straight

Activity 1

Solve.

1. $3\frac{2}{3} + 4\frac{1}{6}$ _____

2. $5\frac{7}{9} - 2\frac{1}{3}$ _____

3. $7\frac{1}{5} + 2\frac{4}{5}$ _____

4. $5\frac{8}{9} \cdot 4\frac{1}{2}$ _____

5. $12\frac{1}{3} - 9\frac{2}{3}$ _____

6. $4\frac{2}{3} \div 1\frac{1}{2}$ _____

Name _____ Date _____

Problem-Solving Activity
More With Tessellations

Make a T template. Then use it to make your own tessellation. You will need a ruler and a protractor. The drawings to the right will help you follow the directions.

1. Use your ruler to draw a 3-inch line on a blank piece of paper. Make two right angles at the ends of the 3-inch line. Do this by drawing 1-inch lines that start at the ends of the 3-inch line.

2. From each 1-inch vertical line, draw 1-inch horizontal lines toward the center of the drawing. These lines should also create right angles. Look at the drawing for help.

3. Draw two more 1-inch vertical lines that start at the end of the horizontal lines. Remember, you are making a T shape.

4. Connect the last two vertical lines you drew with one line. This line should measure 1 inch.

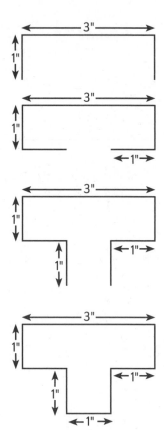

5. Now you are ready to make your tessellation. Begin by setting the T on its side and tracing it in the top left-hand corner of a new piece of paper. Then use your template and protractor to tessellate the shape across the page. When you get done with your tessellation, look for invisible lines that run through the tessellation. These lines and angles are another way of seeing patterns in the tessellation.

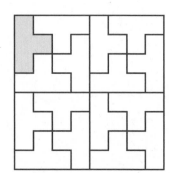

mBook Reinforce Understanding
Use the mBook *Study Guide* to review lesson concepts.

Name _____ Date _____

Skills Maintenance
Mixed-Number Operations

Activity 1

Solve. Remember to use LAPS to organize your work.

1. $2\frac{5}{8} + 3\frac{7}{8}$ _____

2. $5\frac{1}{9} - 3\frac{5}{9}$ _____

3. $7\frac{1}{2} \cdot 8\frac{1}{10}$ _____

4. $3\frac{2}{3} + 5\frac{1}{4}$ _____

5. $6\frac{1}{3} \div 2\frac{1}{2}$ _____

Name _____ Date _____

Problem-Solving Activity
Regular Polygons

Measure one of the angles in each polygon to determine the measure of all of the angles. Then tell the sum of the angles for each shape.

Model	Measure Angle X in the regular triangle. What is its measure? ___60°___ What is the measure of each of the other angles? ___60°___ What is the sum of the angles in this shape? 180° _____

1. Measure Angle A. What is its measure? _____

   What is the measure of each of the other angles? _____

   What is the sum of the angles in this shape?

   _____

2. Measure Angle B. What is its measure? _____

   What is the measure of each of the other angles? _____

   What is the sum of the angles in this shape?

   _____

3. Measure Angle C. What is its measure? _____

   What is the measure of each of the other angles? _____

   What is the sum of the angles in this shape?

   _____

4. Measure Angle D. What is its measure? _____

   What is the measure of each of the other angles? _____

   What is the sum of the angles in this shape?

   _____

Name _____ Date _____

Problem-Solving Activity
Regular Polygons

Draw any polygon on a blank piece of paper. Cut it out and try to make a tessellation with it in the space below. Then answer the questions.

1. Can you make a tessellation with the polygon you chose?

    _____

    _____

2. Explain why your polygon did or did not work.

    _____

    _____

mBook **Reinforce Understanding**
Use the mBook *Study Guide* to review lesson concepts.

Name _____ Date _____

Skills Maintenance
Operations With Mixed Numbers

Activity 1

Solve.

1. $2\frac{1}{4} + 3\frac{7}{8}$ _____

2. $5\frac{7}{8} - 3\frac{1}{4}$ _____

3. $7\frac{2}{3} \cdot 8\frac{1}{9}$ _____

4. $6\frac{7}{8} \div 2\frac{3}{8}$ _____

Name _____ Date _____

 Apply Skills
Approximations and Estimates

Activity 1

Approximate the answers by rounding each mixed number to the nearest whole number. Then solve.

1. $92\frac{11}{14} + 33\frac{1}{88}$ _____

2. $75\frac{17}{18} - 29\frac{1}{4}$ _____

3. $107\frac{22}{33} \cdot 8\frac{11}{12}$ _____

4. $225\frac{2}{3} + 167\frac{29}{30}$ _____

5. $524\frac{7}{8} \div 5\frac{1}{99}$ _____

Name _____ Date _____

✎ Problem-Solving Activity
Approximating Answers to Word Problems With Mixed Numbers

The Scatter Plots is having more problems with the house. Help the band by approximating the measurement problems.

1. The roof on the house leaks everywhere. The entire roof needs to be replaced. What is a good approximation of the area of roof on the front side of the house?

   _____

2. The back side of the house has an extra roof over the porch. What is an estimation of the area of the roof and porch roof on the back side of the house?

   _____

3. The gas pipe to the stove is broken and it needs to be replaced. It comes in under the house and up into the kitchen. About how many feet of pipe does the band need?

   _____

4. The band wants to set up a place to practice in the basement, but there are not enough electrical outlets. The wire will have to be run from the first floor to the basement. The length of wire to the first new outlet in the basement is $20\frac{5}{8}$ feet. The length of wire needed for the second outlet in the basement is $32\frac{3}{4}$ feet. What is the approximate difference between the lengths of the two wires?

   _____

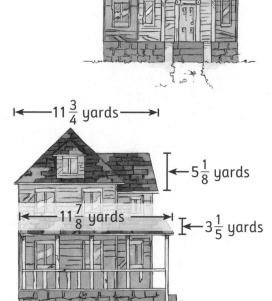

$\leftarrow$ $11\frac{3}{4}$ yards $\rightarrow$

$5\frac{1}{8}$ yards

$\leftarrow$ $11\frac{3}{4}$ yards $\rightarrow$

$5\frac{1}{8}$ yards

$\leftarrow$ $11\frac{7}{8}$ yards $\rightarrow$ $3\frac{1}{5}$ yards

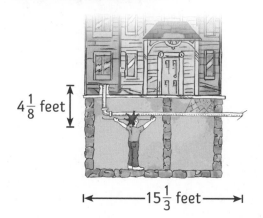

$4\frac{1}{8}$ feet

$\leftarrow$ $15\frac{1}{3}$ feet $\rightarrow$

mBook **Reinforce Understanding**
Use the mBook *Study Guide* to review lesson concepts.

Name _____ Date _____

Skills Maintenance
Mixed-Number Operations

Activity 1

Solve. Remember to use LAPS to organize your work.

1. $43\frac{2}{3} - 35\frac{1}{6}$ _____

2. $22\frac{1}{2} + 16\frac{1}{4}$ _____

3. $8\frac{2}{3} \cdot 2\frac{1}{4}$ _____

4. $12\frac{3}{4} \div 3\frac{1}{4}$ _____

Activity 2

Approximate the answers to the mixed-number problems. You do not need to find exact answers.

1. $37\frac{1}{9} + 59\frac{9}{10}$ _____

2. $157\frac{1}{100} - 64\frac{11}{12}$ _____

3. $4\frac{8}{9} \cdot 8\frac{1}{10}$ _____

4. $17\frac{14}{15} \div 3\frac{1}{50}$ _____

Name _____ Date _____

Problem-Solving Activity
Connecting Circles in Tessellations

Look at the designs with the hidden circles highlighted. Tell if the design is a tessellation of a single regular polygon and if so, tell the angle measurement of the regular polygon.

| **Model** | Is the design a tessellation? (YES)　NO

 If it is a tessellation, what is the angle measurement of the regular polygon? ___60°___ |  |

1. Is the design a tessellation?　YES　NO

   If it is a tessellation, what is the angle measurement of the regular polygon? _____

   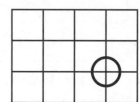

2. Is the design a tessellation?　YES　NO

   If it is a tessellation, what is the angle measurement of the regular polygon? _____

3. Is the design a tessellation?　YES　NO

   If it is a tessellation, what is the angle measurement of the regular polygon? _____

4. Is the design a tessellation?　YES　NO

   If it is a tessellation, what is the angle measurement of the regular polygon? _____

mBook Reinforce Understanding
Use the mBook *Study Guide* to review lesson concepts.

Name _____ Date _____

Skills Maintenance
Mixed Numbers and Improper Fractions

Activity 1

Circle the fractions that are greater than or equal to 1.

$\frac{3}{2}$ $\frac{4}{5}$ $\frac{3}{4}$ $\frac{5}{5}$

$\frac{2}{9}$ $\frac{10}{3}$ $\frac{8}{4}$ $\frac{1}{6}$

$\frac{7}{6}$ $\frac{4}{4}$ $\frac{4}{2}$ $\frac{11}{10}$

Activity 2

Convert the improper fractions to mixed numbers.

1. $\frac{3}{2}$ _____

2. $\frac{7}{5}$ _____

3. $\frac{9}{2}$ _____

4. $\frac{9}{8}$ _____

5. $\frac{4}{3}$ _____

6. $\frac{13}{4}$ _____

Name _____ Date _____

Unit Review
Working With Mixed Numbers

Activity 1

Solve. Use LAPS to organize your work. Show your answer in simplest form.

1. $3\frac{2}{6} + 2\frac{3}{6}$ _____

2. $4\frac{2}{5} + 1\frac{1}{5}$ _____

3. $5\frac{2}{9} + 7\frac{1}{3}$ _____

4. $10\frac{2}{3} - 6\frac{1}{3}$ _____

5. $9\frac{1}{5} - 4\frac{3}{5}$ _____

6. $8\frac{1}{4} - 6\frac{2}{4}$ _____

7. $1\frac{2}{3} \cdot 2\frac{1}{2}$ _____

8. $3\frac{1}{4} \cdot 1\frac{1}{5}$ _____

9. $4\frac{1}{6} \cdot 2\frac{2}{3}$ _____

10. $1\frac{1}{2} \cdot 3\frac{1}{9}$ _____

11. $2\frac{3}{4} \div 8\frac{1}{8}$ _____

12. $5\frac{1}{4} \div 1\frac{2}{9}$ _____

Activity 2

You solved the mixed number problems in Activity 1. Now round the numbers to the nearest whole number to find an approximate answer.

1. $3\frac{2}{6} + 2\frac{3}{6}$ _____

2. $4\frac{2}{5} + 1\frac{1}{5}$ _____

3. $5\frac{2}{9} + 7\frac{1}{3}$ _____

4. $10\frac{2}{3} - 6\frac{1}{3}$ _____

5. $9\frac{1}{5} - 4\frac{3}{5}$ _____

6. $8\frac{1}{4} - 6\frac{2}{4}$ _____

7. $1\frac{2}{3} \cdot 2\frac{1}{2}$ _____

8. $3\frac{1}{4} \cdot 1\frac{1}{5}$ _____

9. $4\frac{1}{6} \cdot 2\frac{2}{3}$ _____

10. $1\frac{1}{2} \cdot 3\frac{1}{9}$ _____

11. $2\frac{3}{4} \div 8\frac{1}{8}$ _____

12. $5\frac{1}{4} \div 1\frac{2}{9}$ _____

Name _____ Date _____

Unit Review
Tessellations, Geometry, and Measurement

Choose one or two shapes and create a tessellation to fill the space in the box. Make sure you use shapes that can be tessellated. Use different colors and try to be creative. After you finish your tessellation, measure the angle seen in the mind's eye.

What is the angle seen in the mind's eye in your tessellation?

_____

mBook **Reinforce Understanding**
Use the mBook *Study Guide* to review unit concepts.

Name _____ Date _____

Skills Maintenance
Fractional Parts on the Number Line

Activity 1

Fill in the missing numbers on the number lines. Follow the pattern.

1.

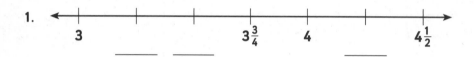

2.

3.

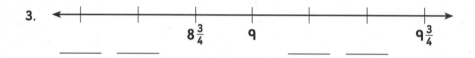

4.

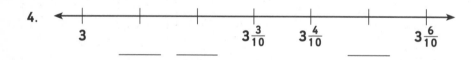

5.

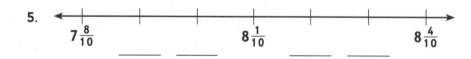

6.

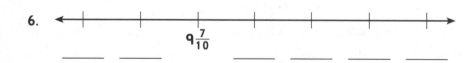

Name _____ Date _____

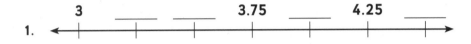

Apply Skills
Decimal Numbers

Activity 1

Fill in the missing numbers. Follow the pattern.

1. 3 _____ _____ 3.75 _____ 4.25 _____

2. 10 10.25 _____ _____ _____ _____ _____

3. 6 _____ 6.50 _____ _____ _____ 7.50

4. 6 6.1 _____ _____ _____ 6.5 _____

5. 7.3 _____ 7.5 _____ _____ _____ _____

Activity 2

Use your calculator to change the fractions to decimal numbers.
Remember, the numerator is divided by the denominator.

1. $\frac{1}{2}$ What is the decimal number? _____

2. $\frac{1}{4}$ What is the decimal number? _____

3. $\frac{3}{4}$ What is the decimal number? _____

4. $\frac{6}{10}$ What is the decimal number? _____

Name _____ Date _____

 Problem-Solving Activity
The Three Parts of a Triangle

Use a metric ruler to make three triangles. Label the three parts of each triangle. Measure the sides using centimeters. When you are done, use a protractor to measure the angles of each of your triangles.

Triangle #1   All three sides must be a different length.

Triangle #2   Two sides of the triangle must be the same length.

Triangle #3   All sides of the triangle must be the same length.

mBook **Reinforce Understanding**
Use the mBook *Study Guide* to review lesson concepts.

Name _____ Date _____

 Skills Maintenance
Decimal Numbers on the Number Line

Activity 1

Fill in the missing decimal numbers and whole numbers on the number lines. Follow the pattern.

1.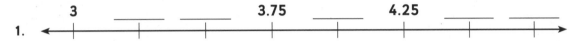

2.

3.

4.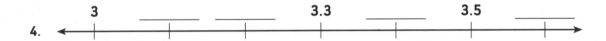

5.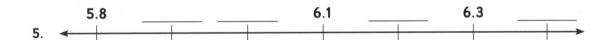

6.

Unit 4

Name _____ Date _____

⅍ ÷ Apply Skills
Fractions With Powers of 10 in the Denominator

Activity 1

Fill in the missing fractions in the equations.

1. $\dfrac{5}{10} \cdot \dfrac{10}{10} =$ ——

2. —— $\cdot \dfrac{10}{10} = \dfrac{70}{100}$

3. $\dfrac{6}{10} \cdot$ —— $= \dfrac{600}{1,000}$

4. $\dfrac{50}{100} \cdot \dfrac{10}{10} =$ ——

Activity 2

Create equivalent fractions by shading the fraction specified in each problem. Then shade the 10-bar box or the 100-box grid to show the equivalent fraction.

1. $\dfrac{2}{10}$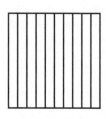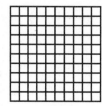

$\dfrac{2}{10}$ $\dfrac{20}{100}$

2. $\dfrac{70}{100}$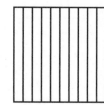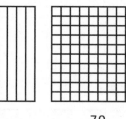

$\dfrac{7}{10}$ $\dfrac{70}{100}$

3. $\dfrac{5}{10}$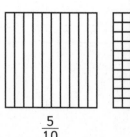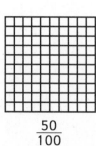

$\dfrac{5}{10}$ $\dfrac{50}{100}$

4. $\dfrac{90}{100}$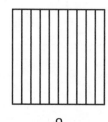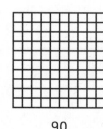

$\dfrac{9}{10}$ $\dfrac{90}{100}$

Name _____ Date _____

 ## Problem-Solving Activity
More Triangles

Use a ruler and a protractor to make three triangles. When you finish each
triangle, make sure that you write the angle measurements for each angle.
None of the sides can be the same length. Remember that all three angles need
to add up to 180 degrees. Begin each triangle with the straight line below. One
angle measurement is given to you.

Triangle #1

Make a 90° angle here.

Triangle #2   Make a 100° angle here.

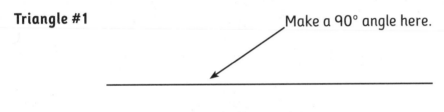

Triangle #3

Make a triangle with three angles that are between 50 and 70 degrees.

---

mBook Reinforce Understanding
Use the mBook *Study Guide* to review lesson concepts.

Name _____ Date _____

 ## Skills Maintenance
Place Value With Whole Numbers

Activity 1

Write the numbers in the place-value tables.

Model	543			
	Thousands	Hundreds	Tens	Ones
		5	4	3

1. 798

Thousands	Hundreds	Tens	Ones

2. 305

Thousands	Hundreds	Tens	Ones

3. 620

Thousands	Hundreds	Tens	Ones

4. 1,044

Thousands	Hundreds	Tens	Ones

Name _____ Date _____

%÷=<x Apply Skills
Writing Fractions as Decimal Numbers

Activity 1

Write the decimal numbers in the place-value tables.

Model

0.27

Thousands	Hundreds	Tens	Ones	Tenths	Hundredths	Thousandths
			0	2	7	

1. 0.54

Thousands	Hundreds	Tens	Ones	Tenths	Hundredths	Thousandths

2. 0.023

Thousands	Hundreds	Tens	Ones	Tenths	Hundredths	Thousandths

3. 1.38

Thousands	Hundreds	Tens	Ones	Tenths	Hundredths	Thousandths

4. 0.009

Thousands	Hundreds	Tens	Ones	Tenths	Hundredths	Thousandths

Activity 2

Change the fractions to decimal numbers.

1. $\frac{2}{10}$ _____

2. $\frac{30}{100}$ _____

3. $\frac{4}{10}$ _____

4. $\frac{500}{1,000}$ _____

5. $\frac{7}{10}$ _____

6. $\frac{80}{100}$ _____

Unit 4

Name _____ Date _____

Problem-Solving Activity
Quadrilaterals

Use a metric ruler to make four quadrilaterals. Use centimeters to measure the side lengths.

Quadrilateral #1   All four sides must be a different length.

Quadrilateral #2   Only two of the sides can be parallel.

Quadrilateral #3   Both pairs of opposite sides must be parallel.

Quadrilateral #4   All four sides must be the same length.

mBook **Reinforce Understanding**
Use the mBook *Study Guide* to review lesson concepts.

Name _____ Date _____

Skills Maintenance
Equivalent Fractions

Activity 1

Fill in the missing numbers to make equivalent fractions in the equations.

1. $\dfrac{5}{10} \cdot \dfrac{10}{10} =$ _____

2. $\dfrac{}{10} \cdot \dfrac{10}{10} = \dfrac{70}{100}$

3. $\dfrac{4}{10} \cdot \dfrac{100}{100} =$ _____

4. $\dfrac{10}{10} \cdot \dfrac{100}{100} =$ _____

5. $\dfrac{65}{100} \cdot \dfrac{10}{10} =$ _____

6. $\dfrac{}{100} \cdot \dfrac{10}{10} = \dfrac{750}{1,000}$

Unit 4

Name _____ Date _____

 Apply Skills
Writing Decimal Numbers as Fractions

Activity 1

Write the decimal numbers as fractions using the graphic organizer.

1. 0.75

Tenths	Hundredths

$\rightarrow \dfrac{}{10} + \dfrac{}{100} \rightarrow \dfrac{}{100} + \dfrac{}{100} = \underline{\quad}$

2. 0.05

Tenths	Hundredths

$\rightarrow \dfrac{}{10} + \dfrac{}{100} \rightarrow \dfrac{}{100} + \dfrac{}{100} = \underline{\quad}$

3. 0.30

Tenths	Hundredths

$\rightarrow \dfrac{}{10} + \dfrac{}{100} \rightarrow \dfrac{}{100} + \dfrac{}{100} = \underline{\quad}$

4. 0.25

Tenths	Hundredths

$\rightarrow \dfrac{}{10} + \dfrac{}{100} \rightarrow \dfrac{}{100} + \dfrac{}{100} = \underline{\quad}$

5. 0.50

Tenths	Hundredths

$\rightarrow \dfrac{}{10} + \dfrac{}{100} \rightarrow \dfrac{}{100} + \dfrac{}{100} = \underline{\quad}$

Activity 2

Rewrite the decimal numbers as fractions.

1. 0.3 _____   **2.** 0.15 _____   **3.** 0.08 _____

4. 0.14 _____   **5.** 0.10 _____   **6.** 0.57 _____

Name _____ Date _____

Problem-Solving Activity
Triangles and Quadrilaterals

Use a ruler or a triangle template to make three quadrilaterals. Begin by drawing or tracing one triangle and then drawing or tracing your next triangle. Use the correct template and then slide, flip, and turn it to create the shapes in the problems.

Quadrilateral #1   Use two right triangles to make a quadrilateral.

Quadrilateral #2   Use two right triangles to make a different kind of quadrilateral.

Quadrilateral #3   Use two isosceles triangles to make a quadrilateral.

mBook Reinforce Understanding
Use the mBook *Study Guide* to review lesson concepts.

Name _____ Date _____

 Skills Maintenance
Converting Decimal Numbers to Fractions and Vice Versa

Activity 1

Convert the decimal numbers to fractions and fractions to decimal numbers.

1. 0.25 _____   **2.** 0.005 _____   **3.** 0.40 _____

4. $\frac{18}{100}$ _____   **5.** $\frac{2}{10}$ _____   **6.** $\frac{52}{1,000}$ _____

Matching

Activity 2

Circle the picture that goes with the term.

1. Parallelogram

2. Parallel Lines

3. Trapezoid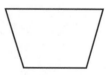

4. Equilateral Triangle

5. Isosceles Triangle

Name _____ Date _____

Apply Skills
Parts We Have and Total Parts of Decimal Numbers

Activity 1

Shade the grids to show the parts we have and the total parts.

1. 0.25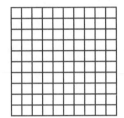

    Parts we have _____

    Total parts _____

2. 0.50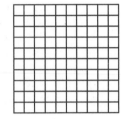

    Parts we have _____

    Total parts _____

3. 0.03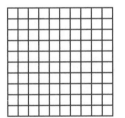

    Parts we have _____

    Total parts _____

4. 0.7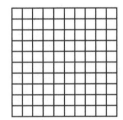

    Parts we have _____

    Total parts _____

Activity 2

Write the fraction for each of the decimal numbers.

1. 0.02   Fraction _____

2. 0.8   Fraction _____

3. 0.003   Fraction _____

4. 0.29   Fraction _____

5. 0.015   Fraction _____

6. 0.090   Fraction _____

mBook Reinforce Understanding
Use the mBook *Study Guide* to review lesson concepts.

Unit 4

Name _____ Date _____

 Skills Maintenance
Part-to-Whole Relationships

Activity 1

For each fraction, tell the parts we have and the total parts.

1. $\frac{25}{100}$ Parts we have _____   Total Parts _____

2. 0.08   Parts we have _____   Total Parts _____

3. $\frac{1}{4}$ Parts we have _____   Total Parts _____

4. 0.25   Parts we have _____   Total Parts _____

5. $\frac{7}{100}$ Parts we have _____   Total Parts _____

6. 0.50   Parts we have _____   Total Parts _____

Name _____ Date _____

 Apply Skills
Zeros In Decimal Numbers

Activity 1

Tell whether the decimal numbers are equivalent by circling yes or no.

1. 0.2   0.20   YES   or   NO

2. 0.5   0.05   YES   or   NO

3. 0.06   0.60   YES   or   NO

4. 0.30   0.3   YES   or   NO

5. 0.04   0.4   YES   or   NO

Activity 2

Convert the decimal numbers to fractions.

1. 0.02 _____

2. 0.1 _____

3. 0.200 _____

4. 0.001 _____

5. 0.010 _____

6. 0.20 _____

7. 0.12 _____

8. 0.012 _____

Name _____ Date _____

Problem-Solving Activity
Reflecting Equilateral Triangles

Trace and reflect equilateral triangles to make quadrilaterals.

Quadrilateral #1 Use the template and reflect it once to make a quadrilateral.

Quadrilateral #2 Use the template and reflect it once to make a different quadrilateral.

Quadrilateral #3 Use the template and reflect it two times to make a different quadrilateral than #1 or #2.

What is the importance of congruence?

_____

_____

_____

mBook Reinforce Understanding
Use the mBook *Study Guide* to review lesson concepts.

Name _____ Date _____

Skills Maintenance
Finding Equivalent Power-of-10 Fractions

Activity 1

Multiply the fractions to find power-of-10 fractions.

1. $\frac{1}{2} \cdot \frac{5}{5}$ _____

2. $\frac{3}{4} \cdot \frac{25}{25}$ _____

3. $\frac{1}{4} \cdot \frac{25}{25}$ _____

4. $\frac{1}{5} \cdot \frac{2}{2}$ _____

5. $\frac{3}{25} \cdot \frac{4}{4}$ _____

Name _____ Date _____

%÷ Apply Skills
=< x Connecting Decimal Numbers With Familiar Fractions

Activity 1

For each problem, sketch the fraction in the blank box. Then sketch the new fraction with the power of 10 on the 100-square grid. Finally, tell what the decimal number is.

1. $\frac{3}{4}$ Sketch the fraction.

$\frac{3}{4} \cdot \underline{\quad\overline{\quad}\quad} = \underline{\quad\overline{100}\quad}$

Draw the equivalent fraction on a 100-square grid.

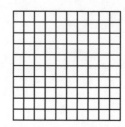

The decimal number is _____ .

2. $\frac{1}{5}$ Sketch the fraction.

$\frac{1}{5} \cdot \underline{\quad\overline{\quad}\quad} = \underline{\quad\overline{100}\quad}$

Draw the equivalent fraction on a 100-square grid.

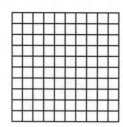

The decimal number is _____ .

Name _____ Date _____

 ## Problem-Solving Activity
Diagonal Lines and Quadrilaterals

Use a ruler and a protractor to divide each of the quadrilaterals into two triangles. Then find the measurement of each angle.

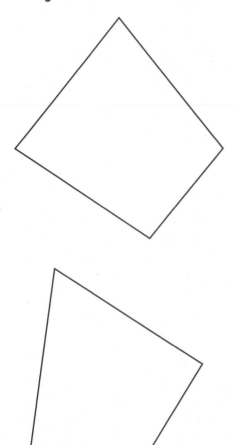

mBook **Reinforce Understanding**
Use the mBook *Study Guide* to review lesson concepts.

Unit 4 • Lesson 7   **151**

Name _____ Date _____

Skills Maintenance
Fractions and Decimal Numbers

Activity 1

Change the fractions to decimal numbers.

1. $\frac{1}{5}$ _____

2. $\frac{3}{4}$ _____

3. $\frac{4}{5}$ _____

4. $\frac{1}{2}$ _____

5. $\frac{4}{10}$ _____

6. $\frac{1}{25}$ _____

7. $\frac{9}{20}$ _____

8. $\frac{2}{50}$ _____

Name _____ Date _____

%÷ **Apply Skills**
Representing Decimal Numbers

> **Activity 1**

Use the circle and the decimal circle to show equivalent fractions and decimal numbers. Use the circle to represent the fraction. Divide the circle into fair shares and shade the fraction. Then shade the same area on the decimal circle and tell the decimal number equivalent.

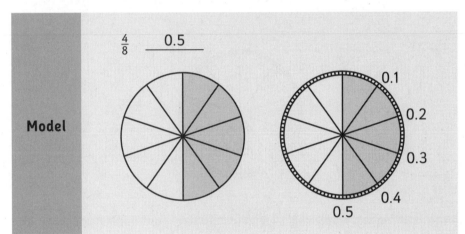

Model $\frac{4}{8}$ 0.5

1. $\frac{3}{4}$ _____

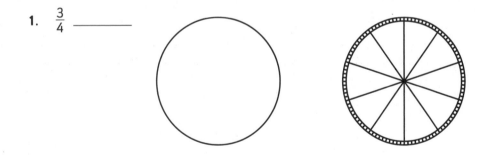

2. $\frac{7}{10}$ _____

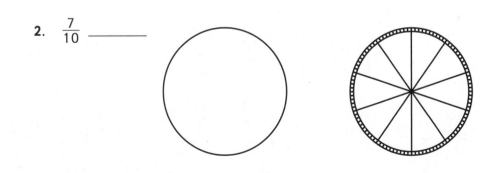

Name _____ Date _____

3. $\frac{1}{8}$ _____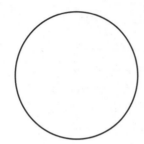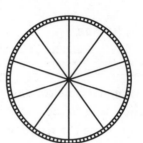

4. $\frac{1}{4}$ _____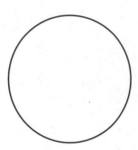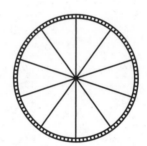

5. $\frac{7}{8}$ _____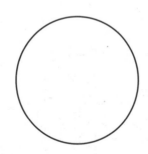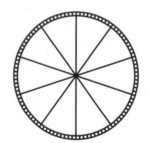

6. $\frac{3}{5}$ _____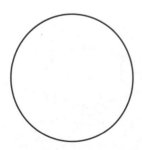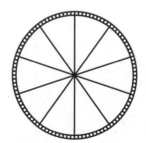

Name _____ Date _____

 Problem-Solving Activity

Classifying Quadrilaterals

Use your ruler and protractor to investigate the properties of each quadrilateral. Make notes that will help you compare the similarities and differences of the four different quadrilaterals.

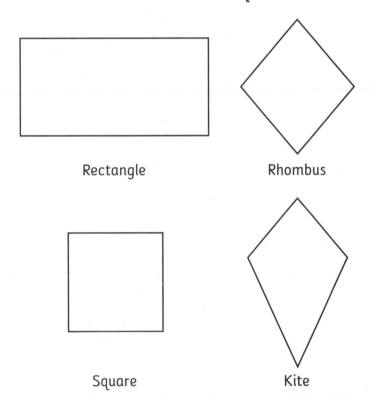

	Alike	**Different**
Rectangle		
Square		
Rhombus		
Kite		

Name _____ Date _____

Problem-Solving Activity
Classifing Quadrilaterals

Draw diagonal lines from one vertex to the other in the quadrilaterals. Then use a ruler and a protractor to measure the triangles that you created. Make sure that you write down the length of the sides and the measure of the angles.

Think about:
- different kinds of triangles (equilateral, isosceles, right, scalene)
- whether or not the two triangles are congruent.

What kind of triangles? _____

Are they congruent? _____

Parallelogram

What kind of triangles? _____

Are they congruent? _____

Square

What kind of triangles? _____

Are they congruent? _____

Rhombus

What kind of triangles? _____

Are they congruent? _____

Quadrilateral

mBook Reinforce Understanding
Use the mBook *Study Guide* to review lesson concepts.

Name _____ Date _____

Skills Maintenance
Writing Fractions as Decimal Numbers

Activity 1

Write the fractions as decimal numbers. Use your calculator to check your answers.

1. $\dfrac{3}{10}$ _____

2. $\dfrac{5}{100}$ _____

3. $\dfrac{55}{100}$ _____

4. $\dfrac{75}{100}$ _____

5. $\dfrac{675}{1,000}$ _____

Classifying Shapes

Activity 2

Circle the correct term to describe each of the shapes.

1.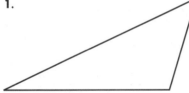

    Acute triangle

    Obtuse triangle

    Right triangle

2.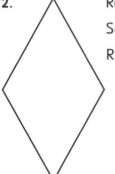

    Rectangle

    Square

    Rhombus

3.

    Scalene triangle

    Equilateral triangle

    Isosceles triangle

Unit 4

Name _____ Date _____

 Apply Skills
Changing All Fractions to Decimal Numbers

Activity 1

Use your calculator to convert the fractions to decimal numbers. Check your answers by using long division.

1. $\frac{7}{8}$ _____

2. $\frac{3}{5}$ _____

3. $\frac{4}{10}$ _____

4. $\frac{9}{8}$ _____

5. $\frac{1}{4}$ _____

6. $\frac{12}{100}$ _____

Name _____ Date _____

Problem-Solving Activity
Changing the Dimensions of Quadrilaterals

Change the properties of the quadrilaterals to make them into different kinds of quadrilaterals. Make sure to measure the sides and angles of the new and old quadrilaterals so you can compare them.

1. square to a rhombus

2. rhombus to a square

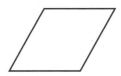

3. parallelogram to a quadrilateral

mBook **Reinforce Understanding**
Use the mBook *Study Guide* to review lesson concepts.

Name _____ Date _____

Skills Maintenance
Converting Decimal Numbers to Fractions

Activity 1

Convert the decimal numbers to fractions.

1. 0.1 _____   2. 0.05 _____   3. 0.100 _____

4. 0.050 _____   5. 0.002 _____   6. 0.300 _____

Relationship of Lines

Activity 2

Circle the correct term that describes each pair of lines.

1. Parallel

   Perpendicular

   Neither

2. Parallel

   Perpendicular

   Neither

3. Parallel

   Perpendicular

   Neither

4. Parallel

   Perpendicular

   Neither

Name _____ Date _____

 Apply Skills
Repeating Decimal Numbers

Activity 1

Use your calculator to convert these fractions to decimal numbers.

1. $\frac{4}{5}$ may be written as the decimal number _____.

2. $\frac{3}{6}$ may be written as the decimal number _____.

3. $\frac{5}{8}$ may be written as the decimal number _____.

4. $\frac{6}{8}$ may be written as the decimal number _____.

5. $\frac{8}{10}$ may be written as the decimal number _____.

Activity 2

Use your calculator to change the fractions to decimal numbers. The answers are repeating decimal numbers. Write the decimal number answer with the line over the repeating part.

1. $\frac{2}{9}$ _____   2. $\frac{2}{3}$ _____

3. $\frac{5}{6}$ _____   4. $\frac{3}{7}$ _____

5. $\frac{3}{11}$ _____   6. $\frac{5}{12}$ _____

7. $\frac{7}{12}$ _____   8. $\frac{11}{13}$ _____

mBook Reinforce Understanding
Use the mBook *Study Guide* to review lesson concepts.

Name _____ Date _____

 Skills Maintenance
Converting Fractions to Decimal Numbers With a Calculator

Activity 1

Use your calculator to convert the fractions to decimal numbers. Remember to write repeating decimal numbers with a line over the repeating part.

1. $\frac{4}{9}$ may be written as the decimal _____

2. $\frac{5}{6}$ may be written as the decimal _____

3. $\frac{2}{3}$ may be written as the decimal _____

Classifying Shapes

Activity 2

Circle the correct term that describes the shape.

1. 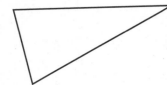   Acute triangle

    Obtuse triangle

    Right triangle

2. 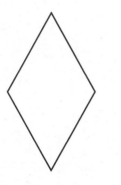   Rectangle

    Kite

    Rhombus

3. 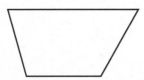   Parallelogram

    Rhombus

    Trapezoid

Name _____ Date _____

 Apply Skills
Ordering Decimal Numbers

Activity 1

Put the decimal numbers in order from smallest to largest.

1. 0.4   0.14   0.04   0.004   Write them in order. _____

2. 0.1   0.02   0.3   0.04   Write them in order. _____

3. 0.098   0.1   0.007   0.02   Write them in order. _____

4. 0.07   0.008   0.29   0.1   Write them in order. _____

5. 0.4   0.75   0.5   0.33   Write them in order. _____

Activity 2

Order the sets of numbers by writing them on different decimal rulers. Remember to put benchmarks at the ends of each ruler before you begin.

1. 4.25, 4.14, 4.3, 4.63

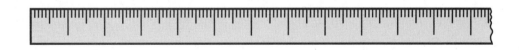

2. 7.92, 7.09, 7.05, 7.5

mBook Reinforce Understanding
Use the mBook *Study Guide* to review lesson concepts.

Name _____ Date _____

 Skills Maintenance
Rounding and Comparing

Activity 1

Round the whole numbers to the nearest 10.

1. 45 rounds to _____ .

2. 32 rounds to _____ .

3. 89 rounds to _____ .

4. 97 rounds to _____ .

5. 129 rounds to _____ .

6. 121 rounds to _____ .

7. 1,349 rounds to _____ .

8. 1,021 rounds to _____ .

Name _____ Date _____

%÷ Apply Skills
Rounding With Decimal Numbers

Activity 1

Round the decimal numbers to the nearest tenth and to the nearest hundredth.

	Nearest Tenth	**Nearest Hundredth**
0.168		
0.157		
0.005		
0.210		
0.099		
0.019		
0.405		

Activity 2

Order the fractions and decimal numbers from smallest to largest.

1. $\frac{1}{4}$ 0.7 $\frac{2}{3}$ 0.5 $\frac{3}{4}$ _____

2. $\frac{4}{5}$ 0.01   0.26   0.9 $\frac{2}{10}$ _____

3. 0.46 $\frac{4}{8}$ 0.8 $\frac{7}{9}$ $\frac{1}{8}$ _____

Name _____ Date _____

 ## Problem-Solving Activity
Trapezoids and Other Polygons

With a ruler, construct shapes from equilateral triangles and trapezoids.
Use the templates for the equilateral triangle and the trapezoid.

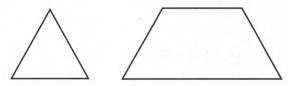

Shape #1   Use equilateral triangles to make a trapezoid.

Shape #2   Use two trapezoids to make a parallelogram.

Shape #3   Use two trapezoids to make a hexagon.

Shape #4   Use equilateral triangles to make a hexagon.

mBook **Reinforce Understanding**
Use the mBook *Study Guide* to review lesson concepts.

Name _____ Date _____

Skills Maintenance
Rounding Decimal Numbers

Activity 1

Round the decimal numbers to the nearest tenths place.

1. 0.45 _____

2. 0.032 _____

3. 0.809 _____

4. 0.097 _____

Activity 2

Round the decimal numbers to the nearest hundredths place.

1. 0.678 _____

2. 0.242 _____

3. 0.515 _____

4. 0.994 _____

Name _____ Date _____

%÷ Apply Skills
=x Finding Decimal Number Benchmarks

Activity 1

Put the list of decimal numbers and fraction benchmarks in order on the decimal ruler. Write each decimal number and draw an arrow to where you think it belongs on the ruler. Then match each fraction to its equivalent decimal number.

0.33   0.75   0.25   0.67   0.5 $\frac{1}{4}$ $\frac{1}{2}$ $\frac{3}{4}$ $\frac{2}{3}$ $\frac{1}{3}$

mm

Name _____ Date _____

 Problem-Solving Activity

Breaking Apart Polygons

Break apart different polygons using triangles and quadrilaterals. Break apart each polygon in two ways. As you complete this exercise, think about which shapes are congruent.

Pentagon

Hexagon

Octagon

Decagon

mBook Reinforce Understanding
Use the mBook *Study Guide* to review lesson concepts.

Unit 4

Name _____ Date _____

 Skills Maintenance
Decimal Numbers and Fractions on a Number Line

Activity 1

Place the decimal numbers and fractions in order on the number lines, estimating their locations.

1. 0.27 $\frac{1}{3}$ 0.1 $\frac{2}{3}$

0   1

2. $\frac{4}{5}$ 0.12   0.01 $\frac{4}{12}$

0   1

3. 0.27 $\frac{1}{3}$ 0.1 $\frac{2}{3}$

0   1

Name _____ Date _____

Apply Skills
Converting Mixed Numbers to Decimal Numbers

Activity 1

Convert the mixed numbers to decimal numbers using a calculator and round to the nearest tenths place. Then place the numbers in order on the number line, approximating their locations.

1. $21\frac{2}{3}$ $21\frac{4}{5}$ $21\frac{6}{9}$ $21\frac{9}{10}$

21   22

2. $72\frac{11}{12}$ $72\frac{3}{4}$ $72\frac{7}{10}$ $72\frac{1}{3}$

72   73

3. $99\frac{1}{4}$ $99\frac{7}{8}$ $99\frac{1}{6}$ $99\frac{1}{2}$

99   100

4. $127\frac{1}{3}$ $127\frac{3}{5}$ $127\frac{1}{10}$ $127\frac{19}{20}$

127   128

Name _____ Date _____

 ### Problem-Solving Activity
Using Properties to Classify Polygons

Classify the triangles and quadrilaterals into groups based on their properties. Use the list of properties to help you. Place the shapes into at least four groups that are not triangles or quadrilaterals.

Properties:

Angles: acute, right, obtuse

Triangles: equilateral, isosceles, scalene

Quadrilaterals: square, rectangle, trapezoid, parallelogram, rhombus, kite

Lines: parallel, perpendicular

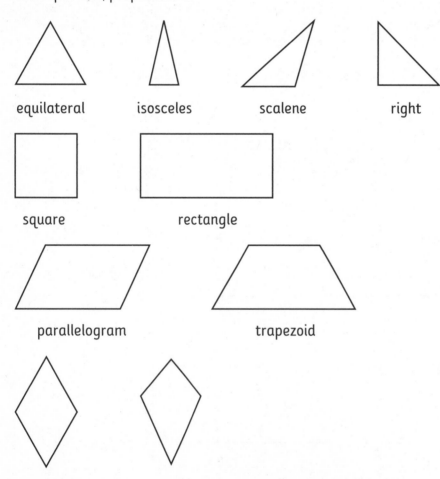

equilateral   isosceles   scalene   right

square   rectangle

parallelogram   trapezoid

rhombus   kite

Name _____ Date _____

Classifying Polygons by Properties	
Shapes in the Group	**Properties of the Shapes**

mBook **Reinforce Understanding**
Use the mBook *Study Guide* to review lesson concepts.

Name _____ Date _____

Skills Maintenance
Relationship of Lines

Activity 1

Write which sides are parallel.

1.

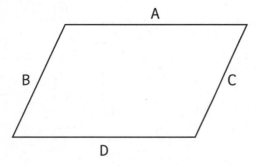

_____

2.

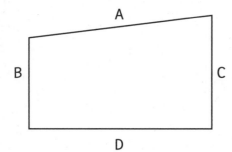

_____

Name _____ Date _____

Unit Review
The Concept of Decimals

Activity 1

Convert the fractions to decimal numbers. Round your answers to the nearest tenth. Then place the rounded decimal numbers on the decimal ruler.

1. $\frac{4}{5}$ _____

2. $\frac{11}{9}$ _____

3. $\frac{3}{6}$ _____

4. $\frac{7}{8}$ _____

5. $\frac{2}{7}$ _____

Activity 2

Estimate the location of the fractions and decimal numbers on the same number line.

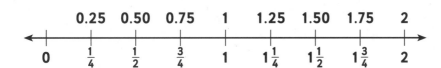

$0.25 \quad \frac{3}{4} \quad \frac{7}{14} \quad \frac{10}{12} \quad 0.09 \quad 0.9 \quad \frac{2}{5} \quad \frac{11}{10} \quad 1.6$

Activity 3

Below are two fractions that seem to be right next to each other on the number line. Use your calculator to convert to decimal numbers and find a number in between. Remember you can add trailing zeros to make equivalent decimal numbers if it helps you understand the numbers better.

1. Name a decimal number between $\frac{6}{8}$ and $\frac{7}{8}$. _____

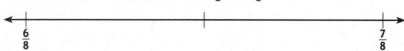

2. Name a decimal number between $\frac{2}{40}$ and $\frac{3}{40}$. _____

3. Name a decimal number between $\frac{19}{80}$ and $\frac{20}{80}$. _____

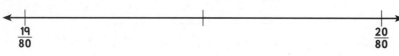

4. Name a decimal number between $\frac{40}{125}$ and $\frac{41}{125}$. _____

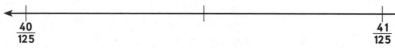

Name _____ Date _____

Unit Review
Triangles and Quadrilaterals

Activity 1

Identify the triangles based on their properties (sides and angles).

1.
    _____

    _____

2.
    _____

    _____

3.
    _____

    _____

4.
    _____

    _____

Activity 2

Use straight lines, reflected shapes, triangles, and anything else you learned in this unit to help you divide the shapes into congruent parts.

1.    2.

3. 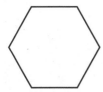   4.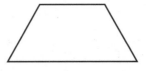

Name _____ Date _____

Skills Maintenance
Ordering Decimal Numbers

Activity 1

Circle the largest decimal number in each list.

1. 0.25   0.2   0.5

2. 0.006   0.060   0.600

3. 0.17   1.7   0.017

4. 1.89   0.189   18.9

5. 0.020   0.2   0.002

6. 0.12   0.09   0.099

Name _____ Date _____

%÷ **Apply Skills**
<=× Adding and Subtracting Decimal Numbers

Activity 1

Rewrite the problems on the sheet of lined paper turned sideways. Use the
lines on the paper to line up the decimal points and the digits. Then solve
the problems.

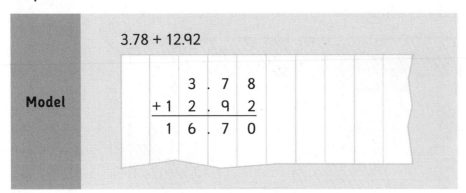

Model   3.78 + 12.92

```
      3 . 7  8
  + 1 2 . 9  2
    1 6 . 7  0
```

1. 2.9 + 4.07 _____

2. 5.62 + 8.7 _____

3. 6.01 + 2.99 _____

4. 2.89 − 1.06 _____

5. 12.6 − 8.78 _____

6. 14.05 − 6.19 _____

Name _____ Date _____

Problem-Solving Activity
The Area of Squares, Rectangles, and Triangles

Calculate the area of the striped section in each shape. Your measurements should be in centimeters. Notice that there are blank shapes inside the shaded shapes. You will need to subtract the area of the inside parts from the larger parts.

1. What is the area of the striped section? _____

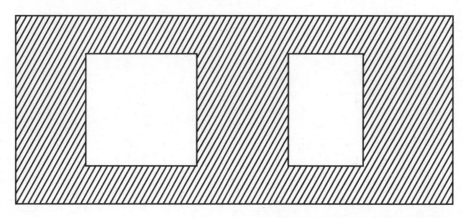

2. What is the area of the striped section?

    _____

mBook Reinforce Understanding
Use the mBook *Study Guide* to review lesson concepts.

180   Unit 5 • Lesson 1

Name _____ Date _____

 Skills Maintenance
Ordering Decimal Numbers

Activity 1

Circle the smallest decimal number in each list.

1. 0.23   0.32   0.032

2. 0.09   0.99   0.900

3. 0.017   1.07   0.170

4. 0.22   0.02   0.20

5. 0.087   0.078   0.87

6. 0.456   0.45   0.650

Name _____ Date _____

Apply Skills
Rounding and Benchmarks

Activity 1

Round the decimal numbers to the nearest fractional or decimal benchmark.

1. 0.27   nearest benchmark is _____

2. 0.78   nearest benchmark is _____

3. 0.48   nearest benchmark is _____

4. 0.99   nearest benchmark is _____

Activity 2

Round the decimal numbers.

1. Round 22.375 to the nearest tenths place. _____

2. Round 72.376 to the nearest hundredths place. _____

3. Round 47.013 to the nearest hundredths place. _____

4. Round 127.557 to the nearest tenths place. _____

5. Add 4.769 + 2.39 and round the answer to the nearest hundredths place. _____

6. Subtract 147.3 − 59.87 and round the answer to the nearest tenths place. _____

Name _____ Date _____

Problem-Solving Activity
The Area of Complex Shapes

Use area formulas for triangles and squares to help you find the area of
the shape in square centimeters.

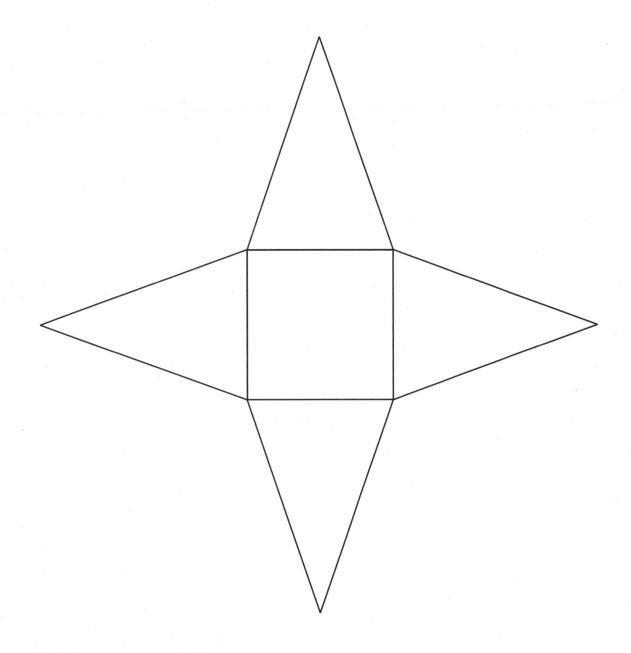

mBook **Reinforce Understanding**
Use the mBook *Study Guide* to review lesson concepts.

Name _____ Date _____

 ## Skills Maintenance
Adding and Subtracting Decimal Numbers

Activity 1

Solve the decimal number problems.

1. 3.75 + 2.1 _____

2. 14.79 − 7.8 _____

3. 18.92 + 22.3 + 14.02 _____

4. 22.97 − 15.09 _____

Finding the Area of Triangles

Activity 2

Find the area of the triangles.

1.
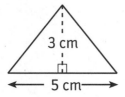
Area _____

2.
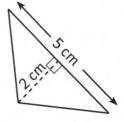
Area _____

3.
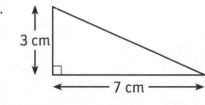
Area _____

Name _____ Date _____

%÷ Apply Skills
<=x Making Sense of Decimal Number Answers

Activity 1

Solve the addition problems. You may use a calculator to find the exact
answers. Then round the numbers in each problem to the nearest whole
number and the nearest tens place.

1.   **Exact Answer**   **Whole Numbers**   **Rounded to 10s**
        16.34   _____   _____
         9.1   _____   _____
        14.785   _____   _____
    +   8.05   + _____   + _____

2.   **Exact Answer**   **Whole Numbers**   **Rounded to 10s**
        23.99   _____   _____
        61.256   _____   _____
        15.1   _____   _____
    + 135.007   + _____   + _____

Activity 2

Write how these answers (exact answer, rounded to whole number, and
rounded to 10s) compare to one another.

_____

_____

_____

_____

mBook Reinforce Understanding
Use the mBook *Study Guide* to review lesson concepts.

Name _____ Date _____

 Skills Maintenance
Working With Decimal Numbers

Activity 1

Round the decimal numbers to the nearest tenths place.

1. 4.78 _____

2. 15.09 _____

3. 12.110 _____

4. 72.005 _____

5. 16.158 _____

6. 27.505 _____

Activity 2

Add or subtract the decimal numbers.

1. 55.7 + 27.99 _____

2. 4.75 + 2.3 + 18.9 _____

3. 17.27 + 2.2 + 5.5 _____

4. 179.2 − 42.85 _____

5. 225.03 − 155.9 _____

6. 307.9 − 299.04 _____

Name _____ Date _____

Problem-Solving Activity
Triangles and Parallelograms

Follow the directions to break the parallelograms into triangles and quadrilaterals. Then use the formulas you know to find the area of each parallelogram.

1. Break the parallelogram into two congruent triangles.

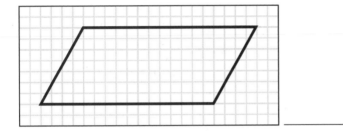

_____

2. Use an equilateral triangle to break the parallelogram into congruent triangles.

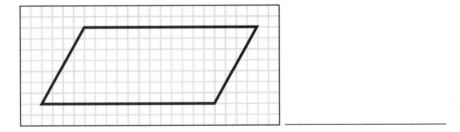

_____

3. Use right angles to break the parallelogram into two triangles and a quadrilateral.

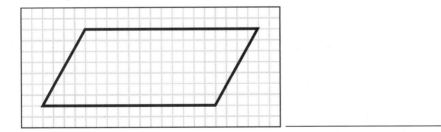

_____

mBook **Reinforce Understanding**
Use the mBook *Study Guide* to review lesson concepts.

Unit 5

Name _____ Date _____

Skills Maintenance
Decimal Numbers

Activity 1

Circle the largest decimal number in each list.

1. 0.5   0.05   0.005

2. 0.72   0.27   0.07

3. 0.22   0.022   0.020

4. 0.12   0.009   0.85

5. 0.75   0.705   0.075

6. 3.9   0.39   0.039

Activity 2

Add or subtract the decimal numbers.

1. 2.37 + 4.9 _____

2. 17.5 − 5.07 _____

3. 15.9 + 22.07 + 32.78 _____

4. 27.29 − 5.8 _____

5. 25.85 + 13.9 + 14.08 _____

6. 223.07 − 119.8 _____

Name _____ Date _____

Problem-Solving Activity
Area of a Trapezoid

For each trapezoid, draw a congruent trapezoid to make a parallelogram.
Then use the area formula for a trapezoid to find the areas of the trapezoids.

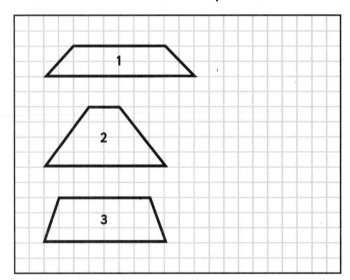

$Area = \frac{1}{2} \cdot (Base\ 1 + Base\ 2) \cdot height$

1. Base 1 + Base 2 _____

   Height _____   Area _____

2. Base 1 + Base 2 _____

   Height _____   Area _____

3. Base 1 + Base 2 _____

   Height _____   Area _____

mBook **Reinforce Understanding**
Use the mBook *Study Guide* to review lesson concepts.

Unit 5

Name _____ Date _____

 ## Skills Maintenance
Basic and Extended Multiplication Facts

Activity 1

Solve the basic and extended facts.

1. $2 \cdot 5$ _____

2. $2 \cdot 50$ _____

3. $2 \cdot 500$ _____

4. $6 \cdot 3$ _____

5. $60 \cdot 3$ _____

6. $600 \cdot 3$ _____

7. $9 \cdot 7$ _____

8. $9 \cdot 70$ _____

9. $700 \cdot 9$ _____

Name _____ Date _____

%÷ **Apply Skills**
≡< X **Multiplying Decimal Numbers**

Activity 1

Use the model to shade the decimal numbers. Rewrite the problem if necessary. Then solve.

Model

0.5 · 0.5
We rewrite the problem:
0.50 · 0.50 = 0.25

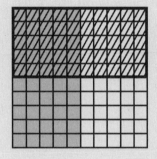

1. 0.2 · 0.5 _____

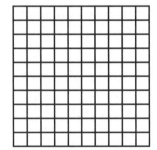

Rewrite the problem and solve.

_____

2. 0.4 · 0.2 _____

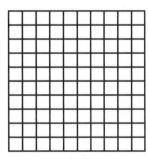

Rewrite the problem and solve.

_____

3. 0.6 · 0.1 _____

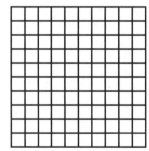

Rewrite the problem and solve.

_____

Name _____ Date _____

Problem-Solving Activity
Areas of Other Polygons

Look at the shapes. Use triangles, quadrilaterals, or both to find their approximate area in centimeters.

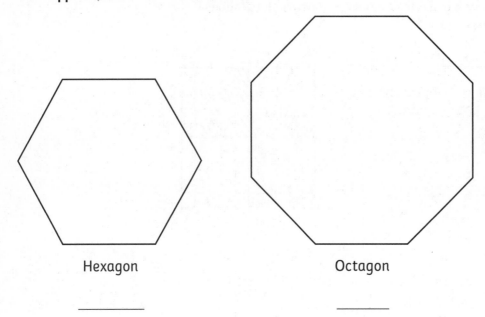

Hexagon   Octagon

_____   _____

 mBook Reinforce Understanding
Use the mBook *Study Guide* to review lesson concepts.

Name _____ Date _____

Skills Maintenance
Rounding to Benchmarks

Activity 1

Round the decimal numbers to the nearest benchmark.

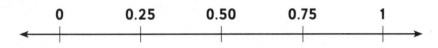

$$0 \qquad 0.25 \qquad 0.50 \qquad 0.75 \qquad 1$$

1. 0.45   nearest benchmark is _____

2. 0.30   nearest benchmark is _____

3. 0.678   nearest benchmark is _____

4. 0.01   nearest benchmark is _____

5. 0.99   nearest benchmark is _____

Unit 5

Name _____ Date _____

%÷=<× Apply Skills
Traditional Multiplication With Decimal Numbers

Activity 1

Multiply the decimal numbers.

1. $\begin{array}{r} 2.21 \\ \times5 \\ \hline \end{array}$

2. $\begin{array}{r} 121 \\ \times 0.40 \\ \hline \end{array}$

3. $\begin{array}{r} 5.02 \\ \times0.2 \\ \hline \end{array}$

4. $\begin{array}{r} 43.2 \\ \times0.2 \\ \hline \end{array}$

5. $\begin{array}{r} 31.2 \\ \times3 \\ \hline \end{array}$

6. $\begin{array}{r} 41.1 \\ \times6 \\ \hline \end{array}$

mBook Reinforce Understanding
Use the mBook *Study Guide* to review lesson concepts.

Name _____ Date _____

 Skills Maintenance
Basic and Extended Multiplication Facts

Activity 1

Solve the basic and extended facts.

1. 3 · 8 _____ **2.** 3 · 80 _____ **3.** 3 · 800 _____

4. 60 · 7 _____ **5.** 6 · 7 _____ **6.** 600 · 7 _____

7. 8 · 9 _____ **8.** 90 · 8 _____ **9.** 8 · 900 _____

Unit 5

Name _____ Date _____

%÷ Apply Skills
Multiplying Decimal Numbers and Number Sense

Activity 1

For each equation, put the decimal point in the right place in the answer.
Think about rounding and estimating as you solve.

1. $0.27 \cdot 8 = 2\ 1\ 6$

    $2.7 \cdot 8 = 2\ 1\ 6$

    $0.27 \cdot 0.8 = 0\ 2\ 1\ 6$

2. $18 \cdot 0.6 = 1\ 0\ 8$

    $0.18 \cdot 6 = 1\ 0\ 8$

    $0.18 \cdot 0.6 = 0\ 1\ 0\ 8$

3. $77 \cdot 0.3 = 2\ 3\ 1$

    $0.77 \cdot 0.3 = 0\ 2\ 3\ 1$

    $0.77 \cdot 3 = 2\ 3\ 1$

4. $0.305 \cdot 0.5 = 0\ 1\ 5\ 2\ 5$

    $30.5 \cdot 0.5 = 1\ 5\ 2\ 5$

    $0.305 \cdot 5 = 1\ 5\ 2\ 5$

Name _____ Date _____

Problem-Solving Activity
Angles, Triangles, and Polygons

Fill in the missing information in the table. Notice the patterns with the number of triangles, number of degrees, and measure of each angle. Use the pictures of polygons to help you.

Polygon	Number of Sides	Number of Angles	Number of Triangles on the Inside	Total Number of Degrees on the Inside	Measure of Each Angle
Triangle	3	3	1	180	180 ÷ 3 = 60
Square					
Pentagon					
Hexagon					
Heptagon					
Octagon					

Triangle

Square

Pentagon

Hexagon

Heptagon

Octagon

mBook Reinforce Understanding
Use the mBook *Study Guide* to review lesson concepts.

Name _____ Date _____

Skills Maintenance
Decimal Operations

Activity 1

Circle the product.

1. $2.3 \cdot 4$

   (a) 9.2

   (b) 0.92

   (c) 0.092

2. $0.17 \cdot 3$

   (a) 51

   (b) 5.1

   (c) 0.51

3. $3.9 \cdot 0.7$

   (a) 27.3

   (b) 2.73

   (c) 0.273

4. $0.79 \cdot 0.1$

   (a) 7.9

   (b) 0.79

   (c) 0.079

Activity 2

Solve the addition, subtraction, and multiplication problems. You may use a sheet of notebook paper to rewrite the problems and line them up. Use rounding and estimating to check your answers.

1. $2.3 + 7.9 + 11.23$ _____

2. $14.7 - 7.89$ _____

3. $21.3 \cdot 0.5$ _____

4. $12.95 + 2.3 + 4.7$ _____

5. $20.19 - 15.5$ _____

6. $3.21 \cdot 0.4$ _____

Name _____ Date _____

Problem-Solving Activity
Perimeters of Regular Polygons and Circumference of a Circle

Find the perimeter of each regular polygon.

1. Perimeter _____

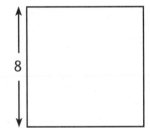

2. Perimeter _____

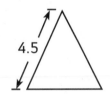

4.5

3. Perimeter _____

◄3.25►

Calculate the circumference of the circles. Round your answer to the nearest hundredth. Use 3.14 for pi. Remember the formula may be written as:

$$\text{circumference} = d \cdot \pi \quad \text{or} \quad \text{circumference} = 2 \cdot \pi \cdot r$$

1. Circumference _____

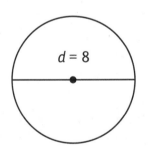

$d = 8$

2. Circumference _____

$r = 0.5$

3. Circumference _____

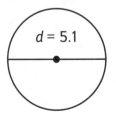

$d = 5.1$

4. Circumference _____

$r = 2$

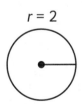

mBook Reinforce Understanding
Use the mBook *Study Guide* to review lesson concepts.

Name _____ Date _____

Skills Maintenance
Decimal Number Operations

Activity 1

Place the decimal point in the correct location in the multiplication problems. Add zeros where necessary.

1. $3.5 \cdot 2 = 7\ 0\ 0$

2. $1.11 \cdot 0.3 = 3\ 3\ 3$

3. $16.4 \cdot 0.5 = 8\ 2\ 0$

4. $0.25 \cdot 3 = 7\ 5\ 0$

5. $5.12 \cdot 0.1 = 5\ 1\ 2$

6. $4.8 \cdot 0.5 = 2\ 4\ 0$

Activity 2

Solve the addition, subtraction, and multiplication problems.

1. $62.12 + 27.89 + 51.6$ _____

2. $134.75 - 73.99$ _____

3. $22.9 \cdot 0.01$ _____

4. $132.9 + 222.89 + 439.07$ _____

5. $230.19 - 135.5$ _____

6. $0.953 \cdot 0.1$ _____

Name _____ Date _____

Problem-Solving Activity
Area of a Circle

Measure the radius for each circle and then use your calculator to compute the circumference and area. Make sure you convert fractions to decimal numbers before you use your calculator. After you calculate each circumference and area, answer the questions.

1. circumference _____

   area _____

   r = 1

2. circumference _____

   area _____

   r = 2

   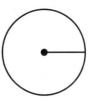

3. Are the numbers for circumference and area ever the same? Why or why not?

   _____

   _____

   _____

4. Is the number for the circumference always bigger than the area? Describe the pattern you see when you answer this question.

   _____

   _____

   _____

   _____

   _____

mBook **Reinforce Understanding**
Use the mBook *Study Guide* to review lesson concepts.

Unit 5

Name _____ Date _____

Skills Maintenance
Basic and Extended Division Facts

Activity 1

Divide the whole numbers.

1. 27 ÷ 9 _____

2. 32 ÷ 8 _____

3. 49 ÷ 7 _____

4. 30 ÷ 6 _____

5. 25 ÷ 5 _____

6. 81 ÷ 9 _____

7. 320 ÷ 80 _____

8. 810 ÷ 90 _____

9. 270 ÷ 90 _____

Name _____ Date _____

Apply Skills
Division With Decimal Numbers

Activity 1

Show division with decimal numbers using the 100-square grid. Begin by shading the number you are going to divide (the first number). Then use boxes to show how many times you can divide the smaller number (the second number) into the shaded grid.

Model

0.8 ÷ 0.4
Step 1: Shade 0.8.

Step 2: Use the number you are dividing by (the divisor) to divide up your shaded area.

Step 3: Write the answer. 0.8 ÷ 0.4 ___2___

1. 0.5 ÷ 0.25 _____

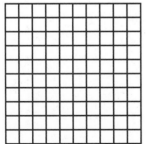

2. 0.9 ÷ 0.3 _____

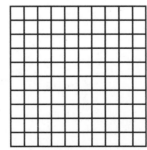

3. 0.6 ÷ 0.12 _____

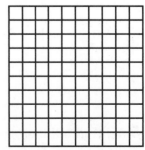

Name _____ Date _____

Problem-Solving Activity
Understanding the Area of a Circle

Now try this activity for yourself. Use a separate piece of paper and a compass.

1. Draw a large circle on your paper.

2. Divide the circle into 16 even pieces.
   - You can do this by dividing the circle into fourths.
   - Then, divide each fourth in half to make eighths.
   - Finally, divide each eighth in half to make sixteenths.

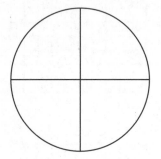 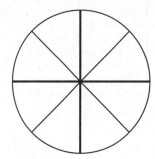 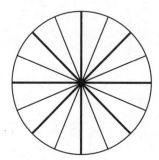

3. Cut out the circle wedges.

4. Lay the circle wedges side-by-side to create a rectangular shape.

5. Measure the height with a metric ruler.

6. Use a calculator to find the circumference and area of the circle.

   Circumference _____   Area _____

mBook Reinforce Understanding
Use the mBook *Study Guide* to review lesson concepts.

Name _____ Date _____

 Skills Maintenance
Decimal Number Operations

Activity 1

Solve.

1. 0.7 + 0.58 _____

2. 0.21 · 0.4 _____

3. 14.98 − 2.8 _____

4. 11.9 · 0.8 _____

5. 1.25 + 2.78 + 3.95 + 8.9 _____

6. 17.89 − 12.9 _____

Name _____ Date _____

⅀ Apply Skills
Traditional Methods for Dividing Decimal Numbers

Activity 1

Solve. Before dividing, move the decimal point right in the divisor to make a whole number. Then move the decimal point the same amount of places right in the dividend.

1. $0.6\overline{)7.2}$

2. $0.04\overline{)2.8}$

3. $0.07\overline{)0.42}$

4. $0.9\overline{)81}$

5. $1.2\overline{)78}$

6. $0.15\overline{)46.5}$

Name _____ Date _____

Problem-Solving Activity
Arcs, Chords, and Semicircles

Use a calculator and follow the steps to find the total area of the two shaded parts in the circle.

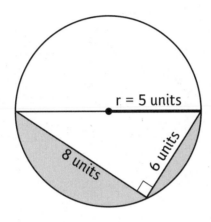

r = 5 units

8 units

6 units

1. Find the area of the entire circle.

    _____

2. Divide the area of the circle by 2 to find the area of the semicircle.

    _____

3. Find the area of the triangle.

    _____

4. Subtract the area of the triangle from the area of the semicircle. This gives us the total area of the shaded parts.

    _____

mBook Reinforce Understanding
Use the mBook *Study Guide* to review lesson concepts.

Name _____ Date _____

 Skills Maintenance
Decimal Number Operations

Activity 1

Solve.

1. 15.5 + 2.78 _____

2. 78.12 − 8.9 _____

3. 14.4 + 22.7 + 18.98 _____

4. 1.21 · 0.2 _____

5. 14.5 ÷ 0.5 _____

6. 18.7 ÷ 0.9 _____

Name _____ Date _____

%÷ Apply Skills
Using Number Sense in Dividing Decimal Numbers

Activity 1

Place the decimal point in the correct place in the answer. Be sure to use good number sense and rounding skills to help you decide the right placement of the decimal point. Add zeros where necessary.

1. $7\overline{)2.457}$ or $2.457 \div 7 =$ 0 3 5 1

   $7\overline{)24.57}$ or $24.57 \div 7 =$ 3 5 1

   $7\overline{)245.7}$ or $245.7 \div 7 =$ 3 5 1

2. $3\overline{)6.51}$ or $6.51 \div 3 =$ 2 1 7

   $3\overline{)0.651}$ or $0.651 \div 3 =$ 0 2 1 7

   $3\overline{)65.1}$ or $65.1 \div 3 =$ 2 1 7

3. $5\overline{)9.85}$ or $9.85 \div 5 =$ 1 9 7

   $5\overline{)0.985}$ or $0.985 \div 5 =$ 0 1 9 7

   $5\overline{)98.5}$ or $98.5 \div 5 =$ 1 9 7

Name _____ Date _____

 ## Problem-Solving Activity
Decimal Numbers in Real Life

The little tags under most items in a store are called unit rates, and they usually tell you how much the item costs by the ounce, pound, or gallon. Think about division as you answer the questions. However, not all of the questions involve division.

1. A 16 ounce can of tomato sauce costs $1.19 and a 24 ounce can costs $1.45. What is the difference in cost between the two cans of tomato sauce? _____

2. You can buy three pounds of chicken for $6.21. How much would it cost for one pound of chicken? _____

3. Potatoes are $0.60 a pound. How much would it cost to buy five pounds of potatoes? You can already buy a five-pound bag of potatoes for $2.30. How much do you save if you buy the five-pound bag instead of buying the potatoes by the pound? _____

4. You are trying to decide what it costs for one can of diet soda. They come in six-packs, and the six-pack costs $2.46. How much does one can cost? _____

5. Hot dogs are on sale. A pound of Yumeez hot dogs cost $2.09 and it is on sale for $1.40. What is the difference between the sale price and the regular price? _____

6. Milk is also on sale. You can buy three gallons of milk for $6.99. How much would it cost for one gallon at this price? _____

mBook Reinforce Understanding
Use the mBook *Study Guide* to review lesson concepts.

Name _____ Date _____

Skills Maintenance
Decimal Number Operations

Activity 1

Circle the correct answer.

1. $1.25 + 2.5 + 3.5 + 1.5$

   (a) 0.875 (b) 8.75 (c) 87.5

2. $27.8 - 17.8$

   (a) 0.10 (b) 1.0 (c) 10

3. $11.2 \cdot 0.2$

   (a) 0.224 (b) 2.24 (c) 22.4

4. $18.2 \div 0.2$

   (a) 0.91 (b) 9.1 (c) 91

5. $2.22 \cdot 0.5$

   (a) 0.111 (b) 1.11 (c) 11.1

6. $27.3 \div 9$

   (a) 0.03033 (b) 0.3033 (c) 3.033

Parts of a Circle

Activity 2

Identify the parts of the circle.

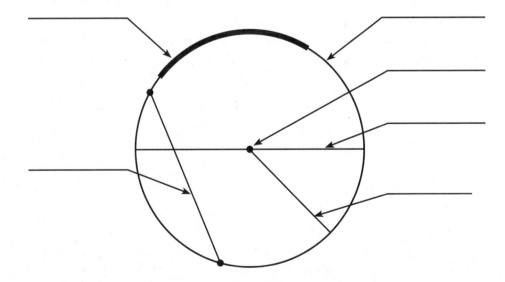

Name _____ Date _____

 Apply Skills
Everyday Decimal Numbers

Activity 1

Round to the hundredths place. Use the number line to find the nearest fraction benchmark. Then solve.

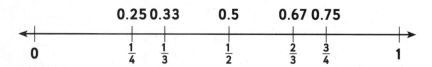

Model	9.325 + 2.311 9.33 + 2.33 It's about ___$11\frac{2}{3}$___ .

1. 25.922 + 5.242   It's about _____.

2. 7.12 · 2   It's about _____.

3. 5.92 ÷ 5   It's about _____.

4. 12.144 + 5.398   It's about _____.

5. 35.95 ÷ 5   It's about _____.

6. 25.022 + 5.22   It's about _____.

Activity 2

Solve the problems based on what you know about fractional and decimal benchmarks. Do the calculations first, then round the answer to the nearest benchmark.

1. William's Auto Parts Company has a machine that cuts rods of steel into smaller lengths. Each rod is 14.42 inches long, and the machine cuts it into 7 pieces called pins. Exactly how long is each pin? About how long is each pin?

_____

2. A relay race involves different runners. As one runner meets the next runner, they pass a stick called a baton. In a recent race, Carmen ran 100 yards in 13.21 seconds and passed the baton to Luisa, who ran the next 100 yards in 13.53 seconds. Exactly how long did it take the two girls to run 200 yards? About how long did it take them?

_____

Name _____ Date _____

Skills Maintenance
Decimal Numbers

Activity 1

Circle the answer.

1. $2.25 + 3.5 + 1.5 + 4.5$

   (a) 1.175 (b) 11.75 (c) 117.5

2. $97.8 - 67.8$

   (a) 0.30 (b) 3.0 (c) 30

3. $19.2 \cdot 0.2$

   (a) 0.384 (b) 3.84 (c) 38.4

4. $8.1 \div 1.5$

   (a) 0.54 (b) 54 (c) 5.4

5. $3.23 \cdot 2.5$

   (a) 80.75 (b) 8.075 (c) 0.8075

6. $36.3 \div 3$

   (a) 0.121 (b) 1.21 (c) 12.1

Activity 2

Solve.

1. $32.12 + 17.89 + 41.6$ _____

2. $254.75 - 62.99$ _____

3. $14.9 \cdot 0.01$ _____

4. $92.9 + 422.89 + 139.07$ _____

5. $210.19 - 35.5$ _____

6. $0.863 \cdot 0.7$ _____

7. $707.9 - 399.04$ _____

Name _____ Date _____

 ## Unit Review
Operations on Decimal Numbers

Activity 1

Solve.

1. Grapefruit cost $1.59 per pound. You decide that you want to buy three. You put all three on the scale and find they weigh four pounds. How much will they cost?

_____

2. Apples are $0.79 per pound or $3.00 for a five-pound bag. How much would it cost to buy five pounds of apples if you bought them at $0.79 per pound? How much would you save if you bought the five-pound bag for $3.00?

_____

Activity 2

You went to the grocery store, the drug store, and the shoe store. Here are the receipts.

🧺 GROCERY STORE	
R E C E I P T	
* * * S A L E * * *	
85520 1 @	14.34
X9X GR 1 @	7.10
550AUT 1 @	4.99
GB09 1 @	11.07
TOTAL	$ 37.50

💊 DrugStore	
R E C E I P T	
* * * S A L E * * *	
RX 1 @	2.89
OXXO 1 @	4.19
8890 1 @	3.66
03AZ 1 @	1.45
TOTAL	$ 12.19

Shoe 👞 Store	
R E C E I P T	
* * * S A L E * * *	
4250 1 @	29.88
XYZ 1 @	3.02
22QY 1 @	30.00
GB 15 1 @	2.33
TOTAL	$ 65.23

1. Approximate a total for each receipt by rounding the prices to the nearest whole number, then adding.

_____

2. Tell why rounding to the nearest tens place would not have been a good strategy to use.

_____

_____

Name _____ Date _____

Unit Review
Area of Two-Dimensional Shapes

Activity 1

Find the area of each shape.

1.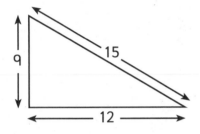

_____

2.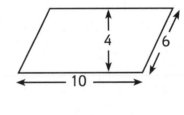

_____

3.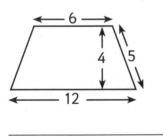

_____

4.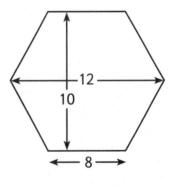

_____

5.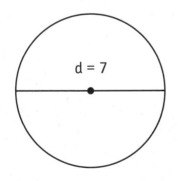

_____

mBook **Reinforce Understanding**
Use the mBook *Study Guide* to review lesson concepts.

Name _____ Date _____

Skills Maintenance
Converting Fractions to Decimal Numbers

Activity 1

Convert the fractions to decimal numbers and vice versa.

1. $\frac{3}{4}$ _____

2. $\frac{3}{10}$ _____

3. $\frac{65}{100}$ _____

4. $\frac{1}{2}$ _____

5. 0.40 _____

6. 0.8 _____

7. 0.25 _____

8. 0.02 _____

Name _____ Date _____

%÷ Apply Skills
Introduction to Percents

Activity 1

Tell the part and the whole for each of the numbers in the table.

Number	The Part is	The Whole is
$\frac{4}{5}$		
0.8		
0.345		
75%		
1%		

Activity 2

For each of the pictures, tell the common fraction, decimal number, and percent equivalent of the shaded region.

1.

Fraction _____

Decimal Number _____

Percent _____

2.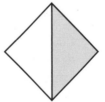

Fraction _____

Decimal Number _____

Percent _____

3.

Fraction _____

Decimal Number _____

Percent _____

Unit 6

Name _____ Date _____

Problem-Solving Activity
Introduction to Circle Graphs

Answer the questions about the data in the table and the graphs on a separate piece of paper.

Survey—What is your favorite pet?		
Type of Pet	Number of People Who Choose this Pet	Fraction/Percent
Cat	6	$\frac{6}{20}$/30%
Dog	10	$\frac{10}{20}$/50%
Hamster	3	$\frac{3}{20}$/15%
Bird	1	$\frac{1}{20}$/5%
Total	20	$\frac{20}{20}$/100%

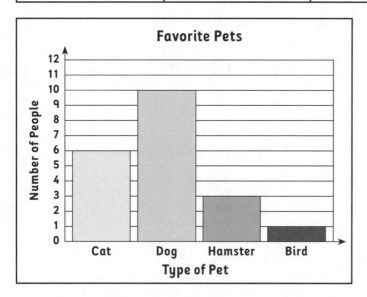

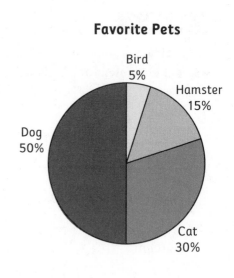

1. If you wanted to tell right away how many people liked dogs, which graph would be the best?

2. If you wanted to compare right away whether more people liked cats than hamsters, which graph would be the best?

3. Write about the different kinds of information you can see in the two graphs. Tell what kind of information is easiest to find in each of the graphs.

Name _____ Date _____

Skills Maintenance
Part-to-Whole Relationships

Activity 1

Tell the part and the whole.

Model	$\frac{16}{100}$ Part ___16___ Whole ___100___

1. $\frac{25}{100}$ Part _____   Whole _____

2. $\frac{5}{10}$ Part _____   Whole _____

3. $\frac{2}{3}$ Part _____   Whole _____

4. 0.49   Part _____   Whole _____

5. 0.2   Part _____   Whole _____

6. 0.02   Part _____   Whole _____

7. 2%   Part _____   Whole _____

8. 45%   Part _____   Whole _____

9. 100%   Part _____   Whole _____

Unit 6

Name _____ Date _____

Apply Skills
Converting Decimal Numbers to Percents

Activity 1

Write the decimal numbers as percents. Remember to move the decimal point two places to the right.

1. 3.29 _____%

2. 0.25 _____%

3. 1.0 _____%

4. 0.01 _____%

5. 0.75 _____%

6. 0.5 _____%

Activity 2

Write the fraction, decimal number, and percent represented by the grid.

1. Fraction _____

   Decimal
   Number _____

   Percent _____

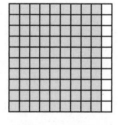

2. Fraction _____

   Decimal
   Number _____

   Percent _____

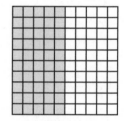

3. Fraction _____

   Decimal
   Number _____

   Percent _____

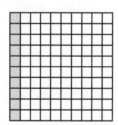

4. Fraction _____

   Decimal
   Number _____

   Percent _____

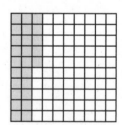

5. Fraction _____

   Decimal
   Number _____

   Percent _____

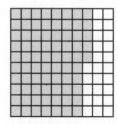

6. Fraction _____

   Decimal
   Number _____

   Percent _____

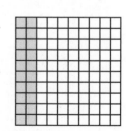

Name _____ Date _____

Problem-Solving Activity
Creating Circle Graphs

Your friend is excited about going to her family reunion this summer. The data in the table shows where her family members live. Create a circle graph to show these data.

Location	Number of People Who Live in This Place	Fraction/Percent
Denver, Colorado	23	$\frac{23}{100}$/23%
Sarasota, Florida	14	$\frac{14}{100}$/14%
St. Louis, Missouri	57	$\frac{57}{100}$/57%
Sacramento, California	6	$\frac{6}{100}$/6%
Total	100	$\frac{100}{100}$/100%

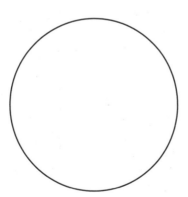

Write two questions and answers about the data in the circle graph.

_____

_____

_____

_____

mBook **Reinforce Understanding**
Use the mBook *Study Guide* to review lesson concepts.

Name _____ Date _____

 Skills Maintenance
Equivalent Fractions

Activity 1

Find an equivalent fraction by multiplying by a fraction equal to 1.

Model	$\frac{3}{4} \cdot - = \frac{}{8}$ Answer: $\frac{3}{4} \cdot \frac{2}{2} = \frac{6}{8}$

1. $\frac{2}{3} \cdot - = \frac{}{9}$

2. $\frac{4}{5} \cdot - = \frac{}{10}$

3. $\frac{6}{8} \cdot - = \frac{}{16}$

4. $\frac{1}{2} \cdot - = \frac{}{18}$

5. $\frac{3}{4} \cdot - = \frac{}{12}$

6. $\frac{5}{6} \cdot - = \frac{}{24}$

Name _____ Date _____

%÷ Apply Skills
Converting Fractions to Percents

Activity 1

Tell the fraction and the percent represented by the shaded portion of each fraction bar.

1. Fraction _____ Percent _____

2. Fraction _____ Percent _____

3. Fraction _____ Percent _____

4. Fraction _____ Percent _____

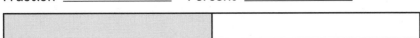

5. Fraction _____ Percent _____

Activity 2

Multiply by a fraction equal to 1 to find the equivalent fraction with 100 in the denominator. Then find the percent.

1. $\frac{25}{50} \cdot \underline{\quad} = \underline{\quad} = $ _____ %

2. $\frac{1}{2} \cdot \underline{\quad} = \underline{\quad} = $ _____ %

3. $\frac{4}{5} \cdot \underline{\quad} = \underline{\quad} = $ _____ %

4. $\frac{10}{25} \cdot \underline{\quad} = \underline{\quad} = $ _____ %

5. $\frac{3}{10} \cdot \underline{\quad} = \underline{\quad} = $ _____ %

6. $\frac{9}{20} \cdot \underline{\quad} = \underline{\quad} = $ _____ %

Unit 6

Name _____ Date _____

Problem-Solving Activity
More Circle Graphs

Create a circle graph. Use the results of a survey of 20 people's favorite type of movie. You may use a calculator to convert the fractions to decimal numbers. Then determine the percent. Draw the circle graph using the decimal circle on the next page.

Favorite Type of Movie	
Type of Movie	**Number of People Choosing It**
Action	7
Drama	4
Science Fiction	3
Romance	6
TOTAL	20

Record the survey results.

Types of Movie	
Movie Type	**Fraction**
Action	
Drama	
Science Fiction	
Romance	
TOTAL	

Use a calculator and convert to decimal numbers, and find the percent.

Types of Movies		
Movie Type	**Decimal Number (from Calculator)**	**Percent**
Action		
Drama		
Science Fiction		
Romance		
TOTAL		

Name _____ Date _____

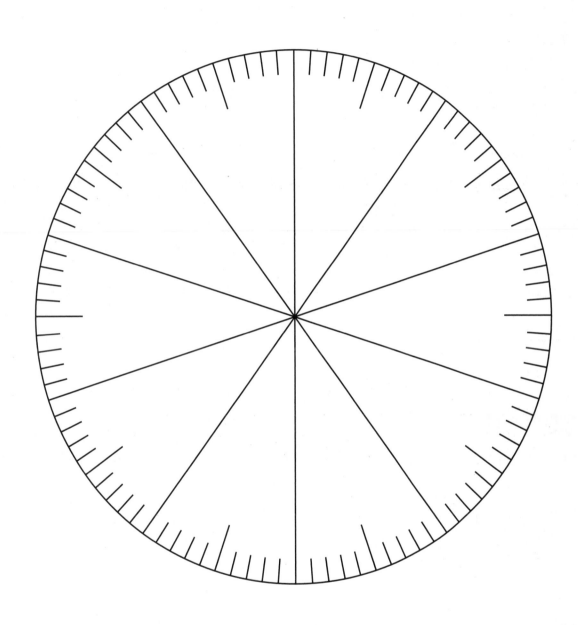

mBook **Reinforce Understanding**
Use the mBook *Study Guide* to review lesson concepts.

Unit 6 • Lesson 3   **225**

Name _____ Date _____

 ## Skills Maintenance
Fractions, Decimal Numbers, and Percents

Activity 1

Fill in the blanks in the table.

Fraction	Multiply by	Equivalent Hundredth Fraction	Decimal Number	Percent
$\frac{1}{5}$	$\frac{20}{20}$	$\frac{20}{100}$	0.2	20%
$\frac{2}{5}$		$\frac{}{100}$	0.4	
	$\frac{20}{20}$	$\frac{60}{100}$		
$\frac{9}{10}$		$\frac{}{100}$		

Activity 2

Write equivalent fractions, decimal numbers, and percents.

1. _____ = 0.25 = _____ %

2. $\frac{1}{10}$ = _____ = _____ %

3. _____ = 0.751 = _____ %

4. _____ = _____ = 100%

5. _____ = 0.034 = _____ %

Name _____ Date _____

Apply Skills
Estimating Percents

Activity 1

Look at the picture in each problem. Estimate the percent of the object that is shaded.

Model

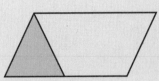

Answer: about 25%
If we were to fill the parallelogram with these triangles, it would take about 4 of them. This is 1 out of 4.
$\frac{1}{4} = 0.25 = 25\%$

1. The shaded part represents about _____ %.

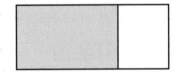

2. The shaded part represents about _____ %.

3. The shaded part represents about _____ %.

4. The shaded part represents about _____ %.

Name _____ Date _____

Draw a percent strip for the percent given in each problem. A percent strip of 100% is provided to help you decide the length of your drawing. Use estimation. You don't need to be exact.

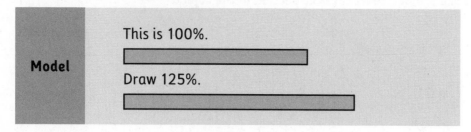

Model

This is 100%.

Draw 125%.

1. This is 100%.

   Draw a percent strip that is about 90%.

2. This is 100%

   Draw a percent strip this is about 150%.

3. This is 100%.

   Draw a percent strip that is about 300%.

Name _____ Date _____

Problem-Solving Activity
Making the Numbers Fit In a Circle Graph

Create a circle graph from the results of a survey of 18 people about what their favorite toothpaste flavor is. You may use a calculator to convert the fractions to decimals. Then round the decimal numbers to the nearest hundredth and determine the percent. You may need to adjust the numbers to make them add up to 100%. Use the blank table and graph on the next page.

Favorite Toothpaste Flavor	
Flavor	Number of People Choosing It
Peppermint	7
Spearmint	5
Cinnamon	1
Wintergreen	5
Total	18

After you create your circle graph, answer these questions:

1. Did you need to adjust the numbers to make them equal 100%?

   _____

2. If you were designing a survey and could survey any number of people, what number of people would you choose?

   _____

   _____

Table 1
Record the survey results.

Toothpaste Flavors	
Flavors	Fraction
Peppermint	
Spearmint	
Cinnamon	
Wintergreen	

Table 2
Use a calculator and convert to decimal numbers, round to hundredths, and find the percent.

Toothpaste Flavors			
Flavors	Decimal Number	Rounded Decimal Number	Percent
Peppermint			
Spearmint			
Cinnamon			
Wintergreen			
		TOTAL	

Name _____ Date _____

Table 3

Adjust the percents if necessary to get 100%.

Toothpaste Flavors	
Flavors	**Percent**
Peppermint	
Spearmint	
Cinnamon	
Wintergreen	
TOTAL	100%

Decimal Circle

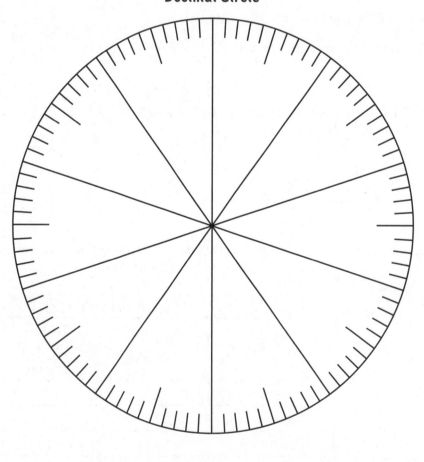

mBook **Reinforce Understanding**
Use the **mBook** *Study Guide* to review lesson concepts.

230 Unit 6 • Lesson 4

Name _____ Date _____

Skills Maintenance
Circle Graphs

Activity 1

Look at the circle graph. Circle the answer to each question.

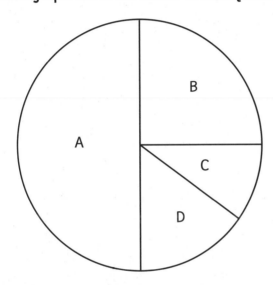

1. Which of the sections of the graph represents 25%?

   A   B   C   D

2. Which section represents 50%?

   A   B   C   D

3. If the topic of the survey for this graph is "favorite foods," which section represents the least favorite food?

   A   B   C   D

4. Two sections together represent 25% of the graph. Which two sections?

   A   B   C   D

Name _____ Date _____

%÷ Apply Skills
Converting Percents to Fractions and Decimal Numbers

Activity 1

Convert the percents to their equivalent fractions and decimal numbers.

1. 25%   Decimal Number _____   Fraction _____

2. 6%   Decimal Number _____   Fraction _____

3. 4%   Decimal Number _____   Fraction _____

4. 65%   Decimal Number _____   Fraction _____

5. 150%   Decimal Number _____   Fraction _____

Activity 2

Solve the discount problems by converting percents to decimal numbers.

1. Discount: 10% off   The decimal equivalent is _____.

   To find the discount, you multiply. _____ • _____ = _____

   To find the sale price, you subtract. _____ − _____ = _____

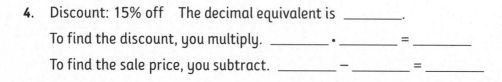

2. Discount: 25% off   The decimal equivalent is _____.

   To find the discount, you multiply. _____ • _____ = _____

   To find the sale price, you subtract. _____ − _____ = _____

3. Discount: 40% off   The decimal equivalent is _____.

   To find the discount, you multiply. _____ • _____ = _____

   To find the sale price, you subtract. _____ − _____ = _____

4. Discount: 15% off   The decimal equivalent is _____.

   To find the discount, you multiply. _____ • _____ = _____

   To find the sale price, you subtract. _____ − _____ = _____

Name _____ Date _____

Skills Maintenance
Discount Problems

Activity 1

Solve the discount problems by converting percents to decimal numbers.

1. Discount: 10% off   The decimal equivalent is _____.

   To find the discount, you multiply.   _____ • _____ = _____

   To find the sale price, you subtract. _____ − _____ = _____

2. Discount: 25% off   The decimal equivalent is _____.

   To find the discount, you multiply.   _____ • _____ = _____

   To find the sale price, you subtract. _____ − _____ = _____

Circle Graphs

Activity 2

Select the circle graph that matches the data.

1. The data set is: 25%, 25%, 25%, 25%.   Which circle graph displays this data?

   (a)   (b)   (c)

2. The data set is: 35%, 35%, 30%.   Which circle graph displays this data?

   (a)   (b)   (c)

3. The data set is: 15%, 15%, 70%.   Which circle graph displays this data?

   (a)   (b)   (c)

4. The data set is: 50%, 25%, 25%.   Which circle graph displays this data?

   (a)   (b)   (c)

Unit 6

Name _____ Date _____

Problem-Solving Activity
Percent Word Problems

Solve.

1. A school's colors are blue and white. There were 500 people at the football game Friday night. If 45% wore blue and the rest wore white, how many people wore blue? How many people wore white?

    _____

2. If a pair of jeans is on sale for 20% off and they cost $70, what is the sale price for the jeans?

    _____

3. Mr. Brown's class of 24 students is going on a class trip to Washington, D.C. Only 25% of the students turned in the permission forms. How many students still need to turn in the forms?

    _____

4. Jane's cereal bar has a food label that says, "150 total calories and only 30% of the calories are from fat!" How many of the calories are fat calories? How many are not?

    _____

Now use the dollar amounts and the percents given to write your own word problems. Be sure they represent real-life situations where percents are actually used. Then solve the problems.

5. Use the dollar amount $180 and the percent 20%.

    _____

    _____

    _____

6. Use the dollar amount $75 and the percent 10%.

    _____

    _____

    _____

mBook Reinforce Understanding
Use the mBook *Study Guide* to review lesson concepts.

Name _____ Date _____

Skills Maintenance
Conversions

Activity 1

Write the equivalent fractions, decimal numbers, and percents.

1. $\frac{2}{3}$ = _____ = _____%

2. _____ = _____ = 8.1%

3. _____ = 0.005 = _____%

4. $\frac{4}{5}$ = _____ = _____%

5. _____ = _____ = 125%

6. _____ = 0.175 = _____%

Unit 6

Name _____ Date _____

%÷ **Apply Skills**
%=× **Percent Increases**

Activity 1

Compute the percent increase for each problem. Change the percent to a decimal number and multiply.

Model	150% of 100	$1.50 \cdot 100 = 150$

1. 50% of 50 _____   **2.** 150% of 200 _____

3. 200% of 300 _____

Activity 2

Find the percent increase for each problem. Draw fraction bars to show the percent increase.

Model

The original amount = 20   An increase of 25%
$0.25 \cdot 20 = 5$ $20 + 5 = 25$

20

5

1. The original amount = 40   An increase of 50% _____

40

2. The original amount = 60   An increase of 20% _____

60

3. The original amount = 70   An increase of 300% _____

70

Name _____ Date _____

 ## Problem-Solving Activity
Making Predictions Using Bar Graphs

Solve the word problems. On a separate piece of paper, draw a bar graph that represents each question. Show the original amount and the answer on each bar graph.

1. Last year, the price of gas was about $2.00 per gallon. The price has increased by 50%. What is the new price of a gallon of gas?

    _____

2. The manager of a shoe store is marking up prices on basketball shoes. She buys new shoes for $50. When she sells the shoes in the store, the price has increased by 75%. What is the store price for the shoes?

    _____

3. After the forest fire, about 40% of the 200 acres of forest had burned. In order to plant new trees, the county wants to know, "How many acres of forest burned?"

    _____

4. Mr. Fine wants to know what will happen if he starts advertising his restaurant in the local paper. The sales people at the paper say he should see a 150% improvement in the number of customers after one month. If Mr. Find currently has about 1,000 customers per month, what should he expect after he starts advertising his restaurant?

    _____

5. The hotter it gets in the summer, the more people go to public swimming pools. The city keeps track of changes in temperature so that it can make sure it has enough lifeguards at its pools. In June, there were about 500 people a day at Coronado Pool. It was much hotter in July, and the number of people per day increased by 300%. How many people were at Coronado Pool each day in July?

    _____

mBook Reinforce Understanding
Use the mBook *Study Guide* to review lesson concepts.

Name _____ Date _____

Skills Maintenance
Fractions, Decimal Numbers, and Percents

Activity 1

Fill in the equivalent fractions, decimal numbers, and percents.

Fraction	Decimal Number	Percent
$\frac{1}{6}$		
	0.33	
		3.5%
	0.029	
$\frac{4}{5}$		
		0.5%
	0.03	
		200%
$\frac{3}{7}$		
		500%

Name _____ Date _____

%÷ Apply Skills
Percents and Benchmarks

Activity 1

What percent do you think each arrow is pointing to on the number line? Your answers will be estimates. Use the benchmarks to decide the percents. Write your answers on the lines provided.

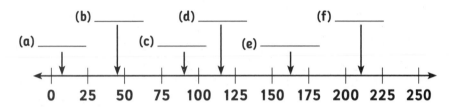

(a) _____   (b) _____   (c) _____

(d) _____   (e) _____   (f) _____

Activity 2

Indicate the closest percent benchmark for the decimal number given in each problem. Use the number line to help you.

Model	0.27 The closest percent benchmark is <u>25%</u>.

1. 0.26   The closest percent benchmark is _____ %.

2. 0.49   The closest percent benchmark is _____ %.

3. 0.779   The closest percent benchmark is _____ %.

4. 0.19   The closest percent benchmark is _____ %.

5. 0.99   The closest percent benchmark is _____ %.

Name _____ Date _____

Problem-Solving Activity
Other Ways to Show Percents

Compute the percents for the numbers in the table. You may use a calculator. Remember to look at the individual numbers compared to the total. Write your answers in the percent column in the table. Use the percents to create a graphic display. You can record the percents under the drawing of the bat.

Look back at the movie ticket graphic in the *Student Text* to help you lay out your graphic here.

Willie Martin's Batting Record		
What Happened to the Batter	**Number**	**Percent**
Home Runs	21	
Singles	38	
Doubles	30	
Triples	12	
Strikeouts	59	
Fly or Ground Outs	40	
Total	200	100%

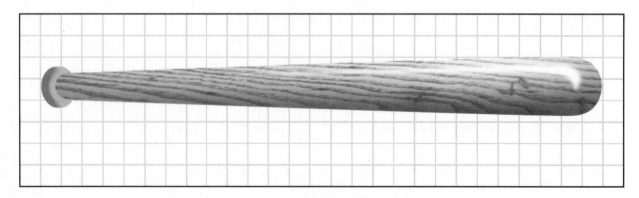

mBook Reinforce Understanding
Use the mBook *Study Guide* to review lesson concepts.

Name _____ Date _____

Skills Maintenance
Fractions, Decimal Numbers, and Percents

Activity 1

Fill in the equivalent fractions, decimal numbers, and percents.

Fraction	Decimal Number	Percent
$\frac{3}{5}$		
	0.055	
	4.35	
$\frac{5}{9}$		
		12.5%
		3%

Activity 2

Use the graphic to answer the questions.

Tabitha's Batting Record

20%
Triples and
Doubles

40%
Singles

10%
Home
Runs

30% Strikeouts

1. What kind of hits did Tabitha get 40% of the time she was at bat? _____

2. What percent of the time did Tabitha get home runs? _____

3. Did Tabitha strike out more than she got hits? _____

Name _____ Date _____

Problem-Solving Activity
Everyday Uses of Percents

Read the word problems. Notice that they contain fractions, decimal numbers, and percents. Solve the problems using any of the methods we used in this unit. You will need to convert all of the numbers to one unit before trying to do any calculations with the numbers. For example, if you want the answer to be a decimal number, you will change all of the numbers to decimal numbers.

1. Breon's homeroom class voted on the color T-shirt they would wear for the next pep rally. The students chose from the school colors: red, black, and white. There are 36 students in Breon's class. $\frac{1}{4}$ of the students chose red. 50% of the students chose black. The remaining 0.25 in the class chose white. What color received the most votes?

   _____

2. Devon is building an obstacle course for her new hamster. She searched through her dad's workshop for scrap pieces of wood. She found a piece of wood that was 12 inches long. She found another piece that was $\frac{1}{4}$ that length. She found a third piece that was 25% longer than the first piece. What is the total length of the wood pieces she found when she laid them lengthwise in a row?

   _____

3. A radio station surveyed 100 of its listeners to determine the time of day the station had the most listeners. The station found that 50% of these listeners tuned in during the 7:00 AM to 9:00 AM time, $\frac{1}{5}$ of the listeners tuned in during the 9:00 AM to 4:00 PM time, and the other 0.3 listeners tuned in from 4:00 PM to midnight. Which time of the day had the most listeners?

   _____

mBook Reinforce Understanding
Use the mBook *Study Guide* to review lesson concepts.

Name _____ Date _____

 Skills Maintenance
Percents, Decimal Numbers, and Fractions

Activity 1

Convert the percents to fractions and decimal numbers.

1. 20%   Fraction _____   Decimal Number _____

2. 50%   Fraction _____   Decimal Number _____

3. 125%   Fraction _____   Decimal Number _____

4. 1%   Fraction _____   Decimal Number _____

5. 99%   Fraction _____   Decimal Number _____

6. 120%   Fraction _____   Decimal Number _____

Activity 2

Solve the problems by changing the percents to decimal numbers and
writing multiplication problems. You may use your calculator to solve the
multiplication problems.

Model	What is 75% of 100? ___0.75___ • ___100___ = ___75___

1. What is 25% of 80? _____ • _____ = _____

2. What is 50% of 160? _____ • _____ = _____

3. What is 10% of 90? _____ • _____ = _____

4. What is 20% of 50? _____ • _____ = _____

5. What is 30% of 200? _____ • _____ = _____

6. What is 200% of 100? _____ • _____ = _____

Unit 6

Name _____ Date _____

 ## Unit Review
Understanding Percents

Activity 1

Identify each number by thinking about nearby benchmarks. You may use fractions, decimal numbers, or percents. Choose what helps you understand the location on the number line the best. Write your answers on the lines provided.

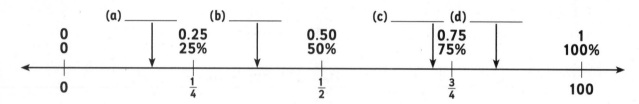

(a) _____ (b) _____

(c) _____ (d) _____

Activity 2

Convert each fraction to a decimal number. Then write each decimal number as a percent.

Fractions	Decimal Numbers	Percents
$\frac{41}{50}$		
$\frac{6}{25}$		
$\frac{110}{100}$		

List the percents in order from smallest to largest. _____

Activity 3

Solve the problem by drawing fraction bars to represent the increase.

1. The price of rice has gone up 8% in the last year. If a large bag of rice cost $25.99 last year, what does it cost this year?

_____

Name _____ Date _____

Unit Review
Percents in Word Problems and Graphs

Activity 1

Select the data set that matches the circle graph.

1.

   (a) 10%, 40%, 2%

   (b) 70%, 50%, 25%

   (c) 12%, 28%, 60%

2.

   (a) 33%, 33%, 34%

   (b) 25%, 50%, 25%

   (c) 50%, 50%, 50%

3.

   (a) 45%, 40%, 15%

   (b) 2%, 100%, 3%

   (c) 12%, 20%, 12%

4.

   (a) 5%, 10%, 15%

   (b) 20%, 30%, 40%

   (c) 25%, 35%, 40%

Activity 2

Calculate each percent increase or decrease. Tell the new price.
Then draw bar graphs on a separate piece of paper.

1. Increase on the price of specialty shoes this year: 35% of $120

   _____

2. Increase on the price of almonds in bulk: 84% of $20

   _____

3. Decrease in price of sweaters for a clearance sale: 75% of $64.99

   _____

4. Decrease on movie tickets for a family because of a 20% off
   coupon: 20% of $29

   _____

Name _____ Date _____

Activity 3

Aaron's mom has four sisters. The table of data shows the number of people on his mom's side of the family, including his immediate family. Complete the table by calculating the percents. Create a circle graph to show the data.

Number of Family Members			
Family	**Number of People**	**Percent**	**Rounded**
Aaron's	6		
Aunt Ashley's	12		
Aunt Amanda's	2		
Aunt Anne's	7		
Aunt Amelie's	3		
Total	30	100%	100%

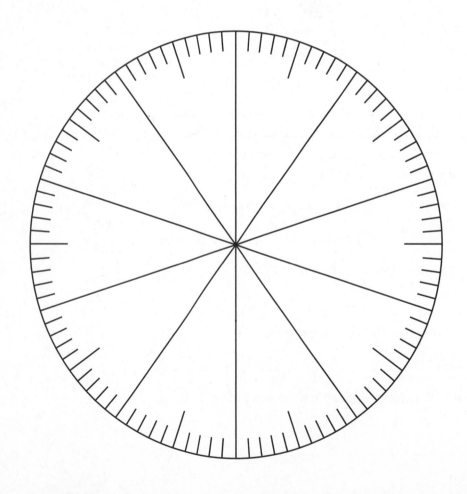

Name _____ Date _____

Skills Maintenance
Fractions, Decimal Numbers, and Percents

Activity 1

Fill in the missing numbers in the table of equivalent fractions, decimal numbers, and percents.

Fraction	Decimal Number	Percent
$\frac{3}{4}$		
	0.7	
		15%
$\frac{1}{2}$		
		1%

Benchmarks

Activity 2

Tell the closest benchmark for each of the numbers. Use the number line to help you.

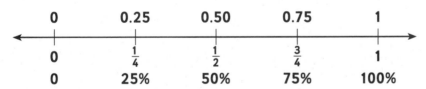

1. 0.39 closest benchmark is _____
2. $\frac{2}{9}$ closest benchmark is _____
3. 99% closest benchmark is _____
4. $\frac{4}{5}$ closest benchmark is _____
5. 19% closest benchmark is _____
6. 0.73 closest benchmark is _____

Name _____ Date _____

%÷=<x Apply Skills
A Review of Powers

Activity 1

Rewrite the powers as repeated multiplication.

1. 3^5 _____

2. 12^3 _____

3. 10^2 _____

4. 2^{10} _____

5. 4^4 _____

6. 4^1 _____

Activity 2

Rewrite the repeated multiplication as powers.

Model	$4 \cdot 4 \cdot 4 \cdot 4$ ___4^4___

1. $3 \cdot 3 \cdot 3 \cdot 3 \cdot 3 \cdot 3 \cdot 3$ _____

2. $10 \cdot 10 \cdot 10 \cdot 10 \cdot 10$ _____

3. $2 \cdot 2 \cdot 2 \cdot 2 \cdot 2 \cdot 2 \cdot 2 \cdot 2$ _____

4. $5 \cdot 5$ _____

5. $4 \cdot 4 \cdot 4 \cdot 4 \cdot 4 \cdot 4$ _____

6. $6 \cdot 6 \cdot 6 \cdot 6$ _____

Name _____ Date _____

Problem-Solving Activity
Probability as a Rational Number

Probability comes into play quite often in the world of sports. How good a player is at something over time helps the coach make predictions about the future. The problems deal with athletes in different sports. Compute the probability for each. Round all numbers to the hundredths place, then write your answer as a percent.

1. Juanita plays guard for the Holton Buzz basketball team. Last season she shot 120 free throws and made 90 of them. What is the probability that she will make a free throw? _____

2. Sheila plays on the same team as Juanita. She's good at three-point shots. In the first 10 games of the season, she took 75 three-point shots and made 25 of them. What are the chances that she will make a three-point shot? _____

3. Benny plays shortstop for the Columbia Jays baseball team. This season he batted 55 times and hit 11 home runs. What is the chance that he will hit a home run? _____

4. Carla is a professional tennis player. Over the last five months, she served the ball 1,000 times. She hit her first serve in 682 times. What is the chance that she will hit her first serve? _____

5. Randy is a wide receiver for the Springfield Mavericks. The quarterback threw 90 passes to Randy last season and he dropped 5 of them. What is the probability that Randy will drop a pass? _____

6. The probability that a professional golfer can make a putt from 2 feet is about 100%. Most professional golfers make about 42 out of 50 putts from 6 feet. What is the probability of a professional golfer making a putt from 6 feet? _____

mBook Reinforce Understanding
Use the mBook *Study Guide* to review lesson concepts.

Name _____ Date _____

 Skills Maintenance
Working With Exponents

Activity 1

Write the repeated multiplication as a power.

1. $2 \cdot 2 \cdot 2 \cdot 2 \cdot 2 \cdot 2 \cdot 2$ _____

2. $3 \cdot 3 \cdot 3 \cdot 3$ _____

3. $4 \cdot 4$ _____

4. $2 \cdot 2 \cdot 2$ _____

5. $3 \cdot 3$ _____

6. $4 \cdot 4 \cdot 4$ _____

Activity 2

Write the powers as repeated multiplication.

Model	2^5	$2 \cdot 2 \cdot 2 \cdot 2 \cdot 2$

1. 5^6 _____

2. 3^3 _____

3. 4^2 _____

4. 2^1 _____

5. 10^4 _____

6. 6^5 _____

Name _____ Date _____

 Apply Skills
Powers and Place Value

Activity 1

Fill in the missing information in the tables.

1. A base of 2

2^5	2^4		2^2		
		8		2	1

2. A base of 4

			4^2		4^0
1,024	256	64		4	

3. A base of 5

			5^2	5^1	5^0
3,125	625	125			

4. A base of 3

		3^3	3^2		
243	81			3	1

5. A base of 10

		10^3		10^1	
100,000	10,000				1

Name _____ Date _____

Problem-Solving Activity
Calculating Chances

Choose a partner and follow the directions to play the game. You need one game board and one scorecard for the two of you. Each of you will also need one item to mark your place on the game board, such as a penny or paperclip. Finally, you and your partner need to choose one item:

1. **a coin (Player 1 = Heads, Player 2 = Tails)**

2. **a deck of cards (Player 1 = Red, Player 2 = Black)**

3. **a die (Player 1 = numbers 1, 2, and 3, Player 2 = numbers 4, 5, and 6)**

You are going to play a game of equal chance. Since only two people are playing, you have a 50% chance of winning. Therefore, we can predict that you will win 5 out of 10 games.

Put one marker on each start. Choose a player to go first. Depending on which item you and your partner chose, on each turn, flip a coin, select a card, or roll a die. If your assigned side, color, or number turns up, you win the round. Move your marker up one place on the game board.

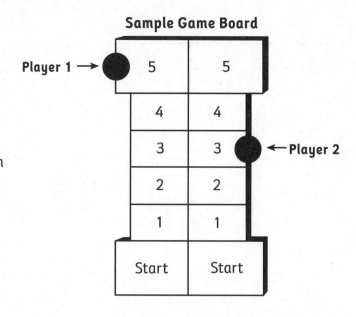

Sample Game Board

The game ends when one of the players lands on 5. Record your scores by figuring out how many total rounds you played, and how many wins each player had. Write this number as a fraction.

For example, if in the first game, player 1 won 5 rounds and player 2 won 3 rounds. 5 + 3 = 8 rounds. So, in the first game, player 1 won $\frac{5}{8}$ of the time and player 2 won $\frac{3}{8}$ of the time.

Play a total of 10 games, recording the scores on the scorecard after each game. Convert the fractions to decimal numbers. Round to the nearest hundredths. After all 10 games, for each player add up the 10 decimal numbers and divide by 10 to find the average.

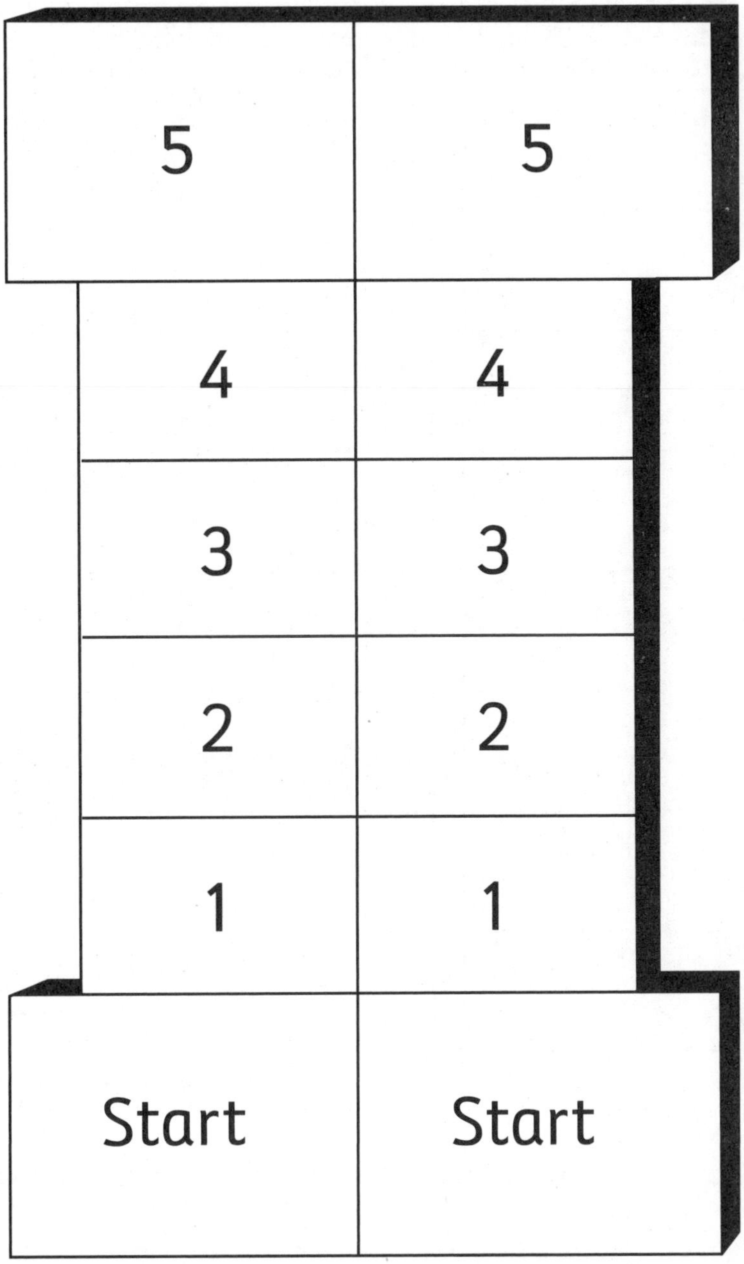

| 5 | 5 |
| Start | Start |

5 5

4 4

3 3

2 2

1 1

Start Start

Name _____ Date _____

Game	Player 1		Player 2	
	Fraction	Decimal Number	Fraction	Decimal Number
1				
2				
3				
4				
5				
6				
7				
8				
9				
10				
Average				

mBook **Reinforce Understanding**
Use the mBook *Study Guide* to review lesson concepts.

Name _____ Date _____

 Skills Maintenance
Working with Exponents

Activity 1

Rewrite the numbers using at least one power.

Model	81 $\underline{3^2 \cdot 9}$

1. 100 _____

2. 49 _____

3. 36 _____

4. 54 _____

5. 32 _____

6. 16 _____

Decimal Numbers

Activity 2

For each of the decimal numbers, tell if it's less than 1, between 1 and 10, or greater than 10. Circle the correct answer.

1. 0.25

Less than 1   Between 1 and 10   Greater than 10

2. 1.5

Less than 1   Between 1 and 10   Greater than 10

3. 6.7

Less than 1   Between 1 and 10   Greater than 10

4. 10.5

Less than 1   Between 1 and 10   Greater than 10

5. 9.8

Less than 1   Between 1 and 10   Greater than 10

Name _____ Date _____

⊞ Apply Skills
Working With Big Numbers

Activity 1

Circle the answer that is correctly written in scientific notation.
Remember to round to the nearest tenths place.

Model	38,400
	(a) $3.84 \cdot 10^2$ (b) $3.84 \cdot 10^4$ (c) $3.8 \cdot 10^4$
	C is the correct selection because it is rounded to the nearest tenths place.

1. 45,000

    (a) $4.5 \cdot 10^2$

    (b) $4.5 \cdot 10^4$

    (c) $45.0 \cdot 10^4$

2. 670

    (a) $6.7 \cdot 10^2$

    (b) $6.7 \cdot 10^3$

    (c) $6.7 \cdot 10^4$

3. 5,890

    (a) $5.89 \cdot 10^3$

    (b) $5.8 \cdot 10^3$

    (c) $5.9 \cdot 10^3$

4. 435

    (a) $4.35 \cdot 10^2$

    (b) $4.4 \cdot 10^2$

    (c) $43.5 \cdot 10^2$

5. 6,810,000

    (a) $6.8 \cdot 10^6$

    (b) $6.81 \cdot 10^6$

    (c) $68.1 \cdot 10^6$

Activity 2

Rewrite each of the distances in the table in scientific notation.

Distance From the Sun to:	Written in Standard Notation	Rewrite in Scientific Notation
Jupiter	460,000,000 miles	
Saturn	938,000,000 miles	
Uranus	1,870,000,000 miles	
Neptune	2,820,000,000 miles	
Pluto	3,660,000,000 miles	

Name _____ Date _____

Problem-Solving Activity
Chance Over Time

In today's problem-solving activity, you will flip a coin a number of times and record the results. Before you start, answer these questions:

1. What is the probability you will flip heads? _____

2. What is the probability you will flip tails? _____

As you flip the coin, put tally marks in each column and calculate the percentage.

	Heads	Tails
4 flips		
10 flips		
20 flips		
30 flips		

Follow these directions for flipping the coin:

1. Start by flipping the coin 4 times. Record the results in the 4 flips row. Use a calculator to find the percentage of times each side of the coin was shown and record the results next to your tally marks. Repeat this process for 10 flips, 20 flips, and 30 flips.

    Are the results what you expected? Explain your answer.

    _____

    _____

    _____

2. If your teacher collected all the data from all the students in the class for 30 flips, what would you expect the results to be?

    _____

    _____

mBook Reinforce Understanding
Use the mBook *Study Guide* to review lesson concepts.

Unit 7

Name _____ Date _____

 ## Skills Maintenance
Exponents and Scientific Notation

Activity 1

Rewrite the numbers using at least one power.

Model	99	$\underline{\quad 3^2 \cdot 11 \quad}$

1. 44 _____

2. 18 _____

3. 25 _____

4. 48 _____

5. 64 _____

6. 144 _____

Activity 2

Match the correct number on the left with the correct scientific notation representation on the right. Draw a line between them.

1. 4,300 $0.43 \cdot 10^1$

2. 43,000 $4.3 \cdot 10^2$

3. 430 $4.3 \cdot 10^3$

4. 430,000 $4.3 \cdot 10^7$

5. 43 million $4.3 \cdot 10^5$

                       $4.3 \cdot 10^4$

Name _____ Date _____

Problem-Solving Activity
What If the Results Are Not What You Expect?

You need two players, two dice, and a score card to play today's game. Decide between the two players who will be Player A and who will be Player B. On each turn, you will roll the dice and find the difference of the two numbers. You subtract the smaller number from the bigger number (or in the case where they are the same number, the number from itself). If the difference of the two numbers is 0, 1, or 2, Player A wins. If the difference of the two numbers is 3, 4, or 5, Player B wins. Keep track of who wins each round for 10 rolls of the dice.

SCORE CARD		
Round	Player A	Player B
Example		X
1		
2		
3		
4		
5		
6		
7		
8		
9		
10		

5 − 1 = 4

After you have played 10 rounds, look at the results.

Are they what you expected? Why or why not?

_____

_____

It seems like there should be an equal chance for the two players to score points. But is that the case? Explain.

_____

_____

_____

_____

mBook Reinforce Understanding
Use the mBook *Study Guide* to review lesson concepts.

Name _____ Date _____

Skills Maintenance
Exponents and Scientific Notation

Activity 1

Rewrite the powers as numbers.

Model	4^5 $\underline{4 \cdot 4 \cdot 4 \cdot 4 \cdot 4}$

1. 2^3 _____

2. 5^2 _____

3. 10^0 _____

4. 8^2 _____

5. 3^1 _____

6. 4^0 _____

Activity 2

Circle the answer that is correctly written in scientific notation.
Remember to round if necessary.

1. 3,000   **(a)** $30.0 \cdot 10^3$ **(b)** $3.0 \cdot 10^3$ **(c)** $3.0 \cdot 10^4$

2. 450   **(a)** $4.5 \cdot 10^3$ **(b)** $45 \cdot 10^3$ **(c)** $4.5 \cdot 10^2$

3. 1,700   **(a)** $1.7 \cdot 10^3$ **(b)** $17.0 \cdot 10^3$ **(c)** $1.7 \cdot 10^4$

4. 4,850   **(a)** $4.8 \cdot 10^3$ **(b)** $4.9 \cdot 10^3$ **(c)** $4.9 \cdot 10^4$

5. 16,000   **(a)** $1.6 \cdot 10^3$ **(b)** $16.0 \cdot 10^3$ **(c)** $1.6 \cdot 10^4$

Name _____ Date _____

Problem-Solving Activity
The Range of Probability

For each of the events, tell the chance of it not happening.

1. If there's a 70% chance of rain tomorrow, what is the chance it will not rain? _____

2. If you are a 60% free throw shooter, what is the chance of you missing the shot? _____

3. If you have a 0.01% chance of winning the raffle at school, what is your chance of not winning? _____

4. What is the chance a coin toss will not land on heads? _____

5. What is the chance you will not roll a 3 on a die? _____

6. What is the chance you will not draw a heart from a regular deck of cards? _____

mBook **Reinforce Understanding**
Use the mBook *Study Guide* to review lesson concepts.

Name _____ Date _____

 ## Skills Maintenance
Exponents and Scientific Notation

Activity 1

Rewrite as powers.

1. $3 \cdot 3 \cdot 3 \cdot 3 \cdot 3 \cdot 3 \cdot 3 \cdot 3 \cdot 3 \cdot 3$ _____

2. $2 \cdot 2 \cdot 2 \cdot 2$ _____

3. 7 _____

4. 1 _____

5. $10 \cdot 10 \cdot 10$ _____

6. $3 \cdot 3$ _____

Activity 2

Select the correct scientific notation for each of the numbers.

1. 580   **(a)** $5.8 \cdot 10^2$ **(b)** $58.0 \cdot 10^2$ **(c)** $5.8 \cdot 10^3$

2. 2,200   **(a)** $2.2 \cdot 10^2$ **(b)** $22.0 \cdot 10^3$ **(c)** $2.2 \cdot 10^3$

3. 17,000   **(a)** $1.7 \cdot 10^3$ **(b)** $1.7 \cdot 10^4$ **(c)** $1.7 \cdot 10^5$

4. 1,300,000   **(a)** $1.3 \cdot 10^6$ **(b)** $1.3 \cdot 10^5$ **(c)** $13.0 \cdot 10^2$

Name _____ Date _____

 Apply Skills
What About Very Small Numbers?

Activity 1

Rewrite the numbers using scientific notation.

1. 0.032 _____

2. 0.0057 _____

3. 0.00068 _____

4. 0.00000012 _____

5. 0.110 _____

6. 0.0000023 _____

Activity 2

Tell what region of the number line the numbers are in. Region 1 includes the numbers between 0 and 1. Region 2 includes the numbers between 1 and 10. Region 3 is anything above 10.

1. $5 \cdot 10^5$ _____   2. $2.6 \cdot 10^0$ _____

3. $3 \cdot 10^{-1}$ _____   4. $2.1 \cdot 10^3$ _____

5. $5.6 \cdot 10^{-5}$ _____   6. $8.9 \cdot 10^{-4}$ _____

Name _____ Date _____

 ## Problem-Solving Activity
When Is it One or the Other?

Today you will look at the probability of winning a common carnival game. You will need a coin toss mat and one coin. Before you play the game, figure out the probability of your coin landing on each type of square.

1. What is the probability of landing on a square with a number?

   _____

2. What is the probability of landing on a square with a letter?

   _____

3. What is the probability of landing on a square with a symbol?

   _____

Carefully follow the steps for playing the game.

1. Select one type of square: number, letter, or symbol.

2. Stand about three feet from the coin toss mat. Toss your coin, aiming for the type of square you selected. Do this 15 times.

3. On the scorecard below, record your results for each of the 15 coin tosses. Write an N if you landed on a number, an L if you landed on a letter, and an S if you landed on a symbol.

Scorecard

1	2	3	4	5	6	7	8	9	10	11	12	13	14	15

How many times did you land on the type of square you selected? Is this close to your prediction?

_____

M	18	★	31
♥	P	44	G
60	▲	S	◆

mBook Reinforce Understanding
Use the **mBook Study Guide** to review lesson concepts.

Unit 7

Name _____ Date _____

 Skills Maintenance
Scientific Notation

Activity 1

Match the number on the left with the correct scientific notation representation on the right. Draw a line between them.

1. 2,700 $2.7 \cdot 10^{-6}$

2. 0.027 $2.7 \cdot 10^{2}$

3. 2.7 million $2.7 \cdot 10^{6}$

4. 0.0000027 $2.7 \cdot 10^{3}$

5. 0.00027 $2.7 \cdot 10^{-2}$

                         $2.7 \cdot 10^{-4}$

Name _____ Date _____

 Apply Skills
Scientific Notation and Probability

Activity 1

Movies make it seem like all kinds of terrible things can happen to anyone at any time. Here are the chances that some common movie events will actually happen to you in real life. Change each of these probabilities into scientific notation.

1. Being hit by an asteroid the size of the one that wiped out the dinosaurs. The chance is 1 in 1,000,000,000 or 0.000000001.

   Write this number using scientific notation. _____

2. A small spacecraft falling from the sky and landing on England. The chance is 1 in 1,700 or 0.00059.

   Write this number using scientific notation. _____

3. Dying in an airplane accident. The chance is 1 in 355,000 or 0.0000028.

   Write this number using scientific notation. _____

4. Dying in a car accident. The chance is 1 in 18,600 or 0.000054.

   Write this number using scientific notation. _____

5. Being attacked by a shark at the beach in the U.S. The chance is 1 in 11,500,000 or 0.000000087.

   Write this number using scientific notation. _____

6. Dying from contact with a venomous animal or plant. The chance is 1 in 3,441,325 or 0.00000029.

   Write this number using scientific notation. _____

7. A meteor landing on your house. The chance is 1 in 182,138,880,000,000 or 0.0000000000000055.

   Write this number using scientific notation. _____

Unit 7

Name _____ Date _____

Problem-Solving Activity
Results of Experiments vs. What is Supposed to Happen

Conduct the experiments with a brown paper lunch bag and two different colors of marbles. You need at least six marbles in the bag and there should be an equal amount of each color. Follow these steps:

1. Shake up the bag to randomly distribute the marbles.

2. Pick a marble without looking inside the bag. Record the color you picked.

3. Put the marble back in the bag and shake the bag again.

Find the chances of pulling out one color first and then the other color of marble from the bag. Make a table to show the possible outcomes and a table to show your actual outcomes.

Possible Outcomes		
First Pull	**Second Pull**	**Outcome**

Predicted outcome _____

Actual Outcomes		
First Pull	**Second Pull**	**Outcome**

Actual outcome _____

How does your experiment compare to the possible outcomes?

_____

_____

Name _____ Date _____

Find the chances of pulling out two of one color and one of the other color, in any order. Make two tree diagrams, one to show possible outcomes and one to show your actual outcomes.

Possible Outcomes

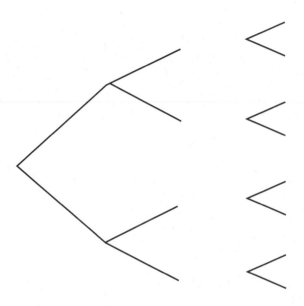

Actual Outcomes

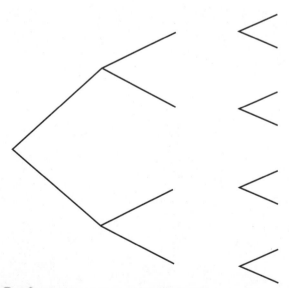

mBook Reinforce Understanding
Use the mBook *Study Guide* to review lesson concepts.

Name _____ Date _____

Skills Maintenance
Multiplying Fractions

Activity 1

Multiply the fractions. Remember to multiply across.

| Model | $\frac{1}{5} \cdot \frac{1}{5}$ $\frac{1 \cdot 1}{5 \cdot 5} = \frac{1}{25}$ |

1. $\frac{1}{3} \cdot \frac{1}{3}$ _____

2. $\frac{1}{4} \cdot \frac{1}{4}$ _____

3. $\frac{1}{6} \cdot \frac{1}{6}$ _____

4. $\frac{1}{2} \cdot \frac{1}{2} \cdot \frac{1}{2}$ _____

5. $\frac{1}{10} \cdot \frac{1}{10}$ _____

6. $\frac{1}{10} \cdot \frac{1}{10} \cdot \frac{1}{10}$ _____

Scientific Notation

Activity 2

Write the numbers using scientific notation.

1. 0.0005 _____

2. 1,300 _____

3. 46,000 _____

4. 0.00000042 _____

5. 45,500 _____

6. 0.000012 _____

7. 0.000371 _____

8. 5,390,000 _____

Name _____ Date _____

Problem-Solving Activity
Multiplication and Probability

Think about drawing cards from three separate decks. The cards are completely shuffled each time and are placed in separate stacks. Use the table that shows the probability of different draws from a single deck of cards. (Remember, the questions are based on drawing from three separate, completely shuffled decks of cards.)

Type of Card	Probability
An ace	$\frac{4}{52}$ or 0.077 or 7.7%
A red card	$\frac{26}{52}$ or 0.5 or 50%
A heart	$\frac{13}{52}$ or 0.25 or 25%
A specific card (e.g., ace of clubs)	$\frac{1}{52}$ or 0.019 or 1.9%
An even number (no face cards included) (2, 4, 6, 8, 10)	$\frac{20}{52}$ or 0.38 or 38%
A face card (J, Q, K)	$\frac{12}{52}$ or 0.23 or 23%

1. What are the chances of drawing the following cards?

    Deck 1   Deck 2   Deck 3

    Red card   Black card   Even Numbered Card

    _____

2. What are the chances of drawing the following cards?

    Deck 1   Deck 2   Deck 3

    2 of spades   five   4 of clubs

    _____

Unit 7

Name _____   Date _____

 Skills Maintenance
Scientific Notation

Activity 1

Each of the numbers contains an error. They were not written correctly in scientific notation. Circle the letter that tells what the error is.

Model	$19.6 \cdot 10^2$ **(a)** the decimal number is not between 1 and 10 **(b)** the base of the power is not 10 The answer is A because the decimal number needs to be a number between 1 and 10. 19.6 is not between 1 and 10.

1. $2.7 \cdot 4^3$

   (a) the decimal number is not between 1 and 10

   (b) the base of the power is not 10

2. $17.9 \cdot 10^3$

   (a) the decimal number is not between 1 and 10

   (b) the base of the power is not 10

3. $44.7 \cdot 10^{-4}$

   (a) the decimal number is not between 1 and 10

   (b) the base of the power is not 10

4. $3.8 \cdot 5^{-3}$

   (a) the decimal number is not between 1 and 10

   (b) the base of the power is not 10

Activity 2

Rewrite the numbers using scientific notation. Remember to round.

1. 0.0008957 _____

2. 5,897,624 _____

3. 0.012798 _____

4. 65,580 _____

5. 0.8968 _____

6. 1,399 _____

Name _____ Date _____

Problem-Solving Activity
When One Thing Depends on Another Thing

Tell the probability of drawing each of the cards after you (a) replace the first card back in the deck, and (b) do not replace the first card back in the deck.

1. You draw a five and then you draw a six.

    (a) Probability if you replace the first card: _____

    (b) Probability if you don't replace the first card: _____

2. You draw a heart and then you draw a club.

    (a) Probability if you replace the first card: _____

    (b) Probability if you don't replace the first card: _____

3. You draw a face card and then you draw another face card.

    (a) Probability if you replace the first card: _____

    (b) Probability if you don't replace the first card: _____

Create a special deck of 10 cards. Four of them should be aces. The rest should be 2, 2, 2, 4, 4, and 7. Make sure that you shuffle the cards so that they are mixed up randomly. There should be an equal chance of pulling out any one of the cards. Then calculate the probabilities for picking different cards in a row. Remember to think carefully about the probabilities for both draws. When you pull out the first card, you are going to put it face up on the table. You will not return it to the deck.

What are the chances of drawing:

1. An ace and then another ace? _____

2. A 4 and then another 4? _____

3. An ace and then a 2? _____

mBook Reinforce Understanding
Use the mBook *Study Guide* to review lesson concepts.

Name _____ Date _____

 ## Skills Maintenance
Fractions, Decimal Numbers, and Percents

Activity 1

Complete the table by filling in the missing numbers. Round decimal numbers to the nearest hundredth. Write fractions in simplest form.

Fraction	Decimal Number	Percent
$\frac{2}{3}$		
	0.24	
		20%
$\frac{8}{11}$		
	0.09	
		35%

Activity 2

Complete the table by filling in the missing numbers.

$3 \cdot 3 \cdot 3 \cdot 3 \cdot 3 \cdot 3 \cdot 3$	3^7
$5 \cdot 5 \cdot 5 \cdot 5$	
	10^6
	4^1
$7 \cdot 7 \cdot 7^5$	
$2^2 \cdot 2^3$	
	13^3
$6 \cdot 6 \cdot 6 \cdot 6 \cdot 6 \cdot 6 \cdot 6^7$	
	8^2

Name _____ Date _____

Unit Review
Scientific Notation

Activity 1

Complete the table by filling in the missing numbers.

Standard Notation	Scientific Notation
3,400,000	**$3.4 \cdot 10^6$**
0.00876	**$8.8 \cdot 10^{-3}$**
545,320	
	$1.2 \cdot 10^7$
0.123	
0.00833	
5,670	
87,001	
	$6.2 \cdot 10^{-9}$
	$9.0 \cdot 10^2$
	$4.0 \cdot 10^5$
0.0000030	
713,000	
0.10005	
	$4.4 \cdot 10^{-2}$
0.0000899	
0.0005612	
	$4.2 \cdot 10^{13}$
0.0109	
0.00000000000005	
	$2.9 \cdot 10^8$
1,999	

Name _____ Date _____

Unit Review
Probability

Activity 1

Sam has 100 marbles in a jar. He counts them by color and keeps a chart of how many he has. Use the chart to answer the questions.

Color of Marbles	Number of That Color
Red	27
Blue	13
Green	10
Purple	31
Orange	19

1. What are the odds of randomly pulling out a blue marble? _____

2. What chance do you have of pulling out a purple marble? _____

3. What color marble are you least likely to pull out? _____

4. What are the chances of picking a red or orange marble? _____

5. What are the chances of not picking an orange marble? _____

Activity 2

You and your friend are playing with five dice. Calculate the chances of each scenario.

1. You are rolling three dice. What is the chance that one die will show a 2? _____

2. Your friend rolled a 1, 6, 2, 4, and 5. What is the chance he will roll a 3? _____

3. Your friend decides to roll for the last time. What are the chances of rolling a 6 with his first die? What are the chances of rolling a 6 with his second die? _____

Name _____ Date _____

Activity 3

Tell the probability of drawing each of the cards after you (a) replace the first card back in the deck, and (b) do not replace the first card back in the deck.

1. You draw a number card and then you draw another number card.

   (a) Probability if you replace the first card: _____

   (b) Probability if you don't replace the first card: _____

2. You draw a king or a queen and then you draw a king or a queen again.

   (a) Probability if you replace the first card: _____

   (b) Probability if you don't replace the first card: _____

3. You draw a seven and then you draw a nine.

   (a) Probability if you replace the first card: _____

   (b) Probability if you don't replace the first card: _____

4. You draw a black card and then you draw a red card.

   (a) Probability if you replace the first card: _____

   (b) Probability if you don't replace the first card: _____

5. You draw a jack of hearts and then you draw it again.

   (a) Probability if you replace the first card: _____

   (b) Probability if you don't replace the first card: _____

mBook Reinforce Understanding
Use the mBook *Study Guide* to review unit concepts.

Name _____ Date _____

Skills Maintenance
Rational Numbers

Activity 1

Fill in the missing rational numbers in the table of equivalents. The first row is done for you.

Fraction	Decimal Number	Percent
$\frac{3}{4}$	0.75	75%
	0.50	
		25%
$\frac{4}{5}$		
	0.7	
		1%
$\frac{1}{10}$		
	0.08	
		0.5%
$\frac{3}{100}$		
	0.006	
		3.5%
$\frac{1}{5}$		
	1.5	
		100%

Name _____ Date _____

Apply Skills
Negatives and Opposites

Activity 1

Name the missing numbers on the number lines. Remember the idea of symmetry on the number line and look at the opposites on the other side of zero to help name the missing numbers.

1.

    -50   -40   -30   -20   -10   0   (a)   (b)   (c)   (d)   (e)

2.

    $-1\frac{1}{4}$ -1 $-\frac{3}{4}$ $-\frac{1}{2}$ $-\frac{1}{4}$ 0   (a)   (b)   (c)   (d)   (e)

3.

    -5   -4   -3   -2   -1   0   (a)   (b)   (c)   (d)   (e)

4.

    -25   -20   -15   -10   -5   0   (a)   (b)   (c)   (d)   (e)

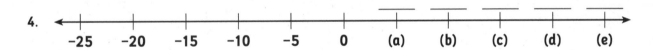

Activity 2

Write the opposite in each problem. Use the number lines above and your knowledge of symmetry.

1. The opposite of 2 is _____ .

2. The opposite of −20 is _____ .

3. The opposite of −5 is _____ .

4. The opposite of 10 is _____ .

5. The opposite of 30 is _____ .

6. The opposite of −7 is _____ .

Unit 8

Name _____ Date _____

Problem-Solving Activity
Bar Graphs

Use the information in the bar graph to answer the questions about Jamaal's football practice. You may use a calculator. As you answer the questions, assume Jamaal's practice record showed only whole hours without any extra minutes.

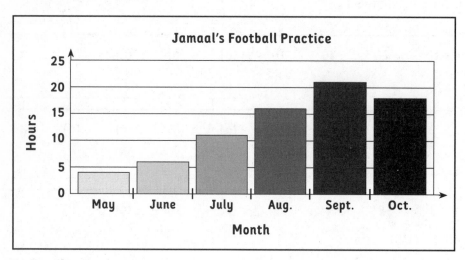

1. About how many hours did Jamaal practice each month from May through October?

    May _____   June _____

    July _____   August _____

    September _____   October _____

2. In what month did he practice the most? _____

3. In what month did he practice the least? _____

4. What is the range in hours that Jamaal practiced football in the six months from May through October? _____

5. What is the average number of hours per month that Jamaal practiced football between May and October? _____

mBook **Reinforce Understanding**
Use the mBook *Study Guide* to review lesson concepts.

Name _____ Date _____

 Skills Maintenance
Identifying Opposites

Activity 1

Complete the statements about opposites.

1. 100 is the opposite of _____ .

2. −3 is the opposite of _____ .

3. 40 is the opposite of _____ .

4. −35 is the opposite of _____ .

5. 24 is the opposite of _____ .

6. −9 is the opposite of _____ .

Bar Graphs

Activity 2

Use the bar graph to answer the questions. Circle your answer.

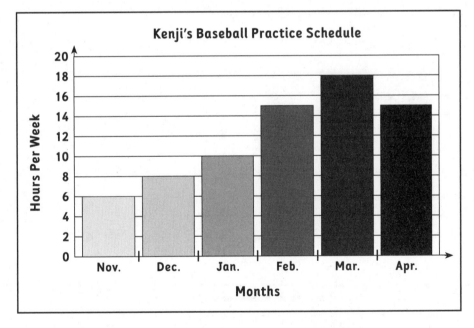

1. What is the label on the x-axis?

   (a) Hours Per Week

   (b) Months

   (c) Kenji's Baseball Practice Schedule

2. When did Kenji practice the most?

   (a) Nov.

   (b) April

   (c) Mar.

3. What is the label on the y-axis?

   (a) Hours Per Week

   (b) Months

   (c) Kenji's Baseball Practice Schedule

Unit 8

Name _____ Date _____

%÷ Apply Skills
<÷x Representing Change on the Number Line

Activity 1

Complete the statements using number lines. The dashed line shows a negative direction.

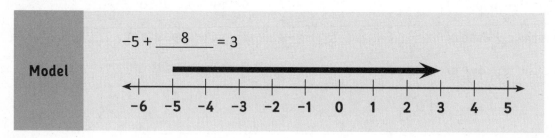

Model

$-5 +$ ___8___ $= 3$

1. $-4 +$ _____ $= -3$

2. $1 -$ _____ $= -4$

3. $-6 +$ _____ $= 3$

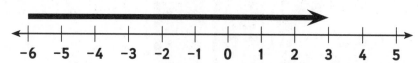

4. $1 +$ _____ $= 5$

mBook Reinforce Understanding
Use the mBook *Study Guide* to review lesson concepts.

Name _____ Date _____

Skills Maintenance
Representing Change on the Number Line

Activity 1

Complete the statements using number lines. The dashed lines show a negative direction.

1. $-2 -$ _____ $= -6$

2. $5 -$ _____ $= 1$

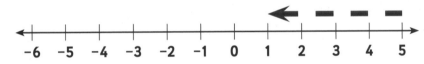

3. $-2 +$ _____ $= 2$

4. $1 -$ _____ $= -4$

Unit 8

Name _____ Date _____

%÷ Apply Skills
<= Using Integers
< X

Activity 1

Tell how much of a change occurred and circle whether it was positive or negative in each of the problems.

1.

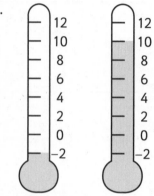

What is the change? _____

In which direction? (circle one)

POSITIVE   or   NEGATIVE

2.

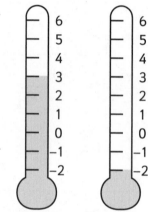

What is the change? _____

In which direction? (circle one)

POSITIVE   or   NEGATIVE

3.

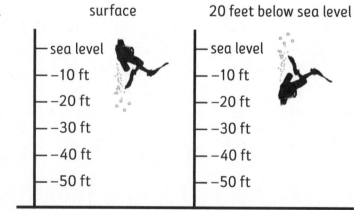

What is the change? _____

In which direction? (circle one)   POSITIVE   or   NEGATIVE

Name _____ Date _____

Problem-Solving Activity
Negative Numbers in Bar Graphs

Construct a bar graph based on the data in the table. Include the necessary elements for a graph: title, labels for the *x*- and *y*-axis,and correct integer values on the vertical axis.

Al's Lawn and Yard Service mows lawns and does other yard work. Al's business makes different amounts of money depending on the time of year. He loses money during the winter when it is cold and there is snow on the ground. While he has a few jobs, Al's business still loses money because what he pays his workers and what it costs to fix his equipment is more than what he makes during those months.

Al's Lawn and Yard Service: Monthly Income	
Month	**Monthly Income**
January	−500
February	−450
March	−100
April	200
May	500
June	750
July	800

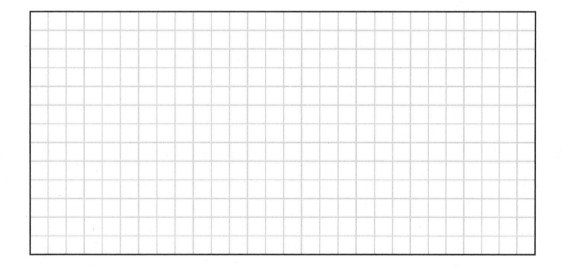

mBook **Reinforce Understanding**
Use the **mBook** *Study Guide* to review lesson concepts.

Unit 8 • Lesson 3   **285**

Unit 8

Name _____ Date _____

 Skills Maintenance
Identifying Opposites

Activity 1

Write the opposite for each of the numbers. Then circle the larger number.

1. −30 _____

2. 62 _____

3. 1,010 _____

4. −1 _____

5. 45 _____

6. −100 _____

7. 100,000,000 _____

8. 4 _____

Name _____ Date _____

⚎ Apply Skills
Comparing Integers

Activity 1

Write the correct symbol (> or <) to make each of the statements true.

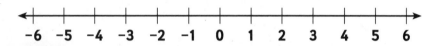

| **Model** | −5 ___<___ 1 |

1. −4 _____ −5

2. 1 _____ −5

3. −6 _____ −5

4. 2 _____ −2

5. −6 _____ 0

6. −3 _____ −1

7. 0 _____ −6

8. −4 _____ −3

Activity 2

Circle whether each statement is True or False.

1. −3 > −2   True   or   False

2. −1 < −5   True   or   False

3. 0 > −7   True   or   False

4. 3 < −10   True   or   False

5. −4 < −3   True   or   False

6. −1 > 0   True   or   False

7. 10 > 5   True   or   False

8. −10 > −5   True   or   False

Unit 8

Name _____ Date _____

Problem-Solving Activity
Dot Graphs

The lead singer of the Scatter Plots wants to collect information on how many people send him fan mail per week. Use the information in the table to create a dot graph, then answer the questions.

Week	Pieces of Mail
1	35
2	12
3	100
4	47
5	5
6	23
7	20

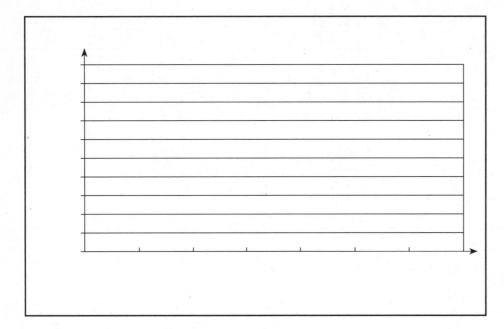

1. Why do we use a dot graph in this situation?

   _____

   _____

2. During which week did the lead singer receive the most mail? _____

   The least mail? _____

3. What is the range of mail the lead singer received? _____

mBook Reinforce Understanding
Use the mBook *Study Guide* to review lesson concepts.

Name _____ Date _____

Skills Maintenance
Comparing Positive and Negative Integers

Activity 1

Use the number line provided to help compare the two numbers.
Write > or <.

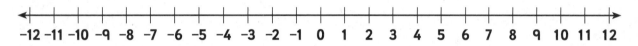

1. −2 _____ −1

2. 0 _____ −1

3. 5 _____ −5

4. −5 _____ −4

5. 4 _____ 3

6. −2 _____ −3

7. −10 _____ −9

8. −4 _____ 0

Unit 8

Name _____ Date _____

%÷ Apply Skills
≥< x Adding Positive and Negative Integers

Activity 1

Solve the addition problems using the number lines. Draw negative arrows in red. Draw positive arrows in black.

1. −3 + −4 _____

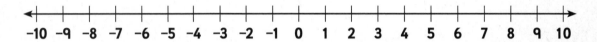

2. −1 + 8 _____

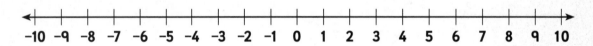

3. 4 + −4 _____

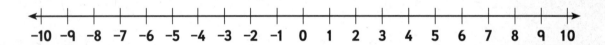

Activity 2

Write the equation shown on each number line. Remember to start at zero each time.

1.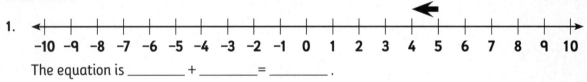

The equation is _____ + _____ = _____ .

2.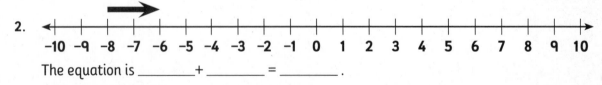

The equation is _____ + _____ = _____ .

3.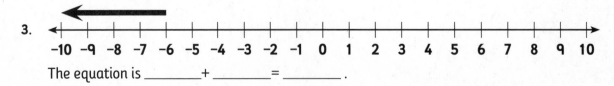

The equation is _____ + _____ = _____ .

Name _____ Date _____

Skills Maintenance
Adding Positive and Negative Numbers

Activity 1

Solve the addition problems using the number lines. Remember to use red pen or pencil to draw the negative arrows and black pen or pencil to draw the positive arrows.

1. 10 + −5 _____

2. −6 + −2 _____

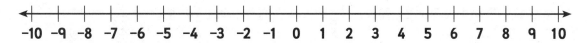

3. −8 + 8 _____

4. 5 + −6 _____

5. 0 + −7 _____

6. −2 + 4 _____

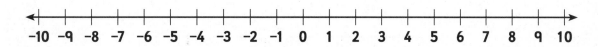

Unit 8

Name _____ Date _____

Apply Skills
Another Way of Looking at Integer Addition

Activity 1

Solve the addition problems. Use the red and black cards.

Note: In the *Interactive Text*, red cards are gray cards.

1. $-3 + 2$ _____

2. $-4 + 4$ _____

3. $10 + -7$ _____

4. $6 + -7$ _____

Activity 2

Use the number line to show how you can cancel out a red card with a black card. Then explain why the process of canceling out works.

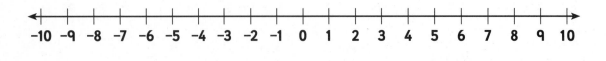

_____

_____

_____

Name _____ Date _____

Problem-Solving Activity
More Dot Graphs

Matt watches his little brother each week. He makes $15 per week for this job. Matt is saving his money to buy the latest video game, SW Raiders, and the controller. The table shows how much money Matt has in his bank account for every two weeks. Look at the table and the dot graph, then answer the questions.

Week	Money in Matt's Bank Account
2	$30
4	$60
6	$90
8	−$30
10	$0
12	$30

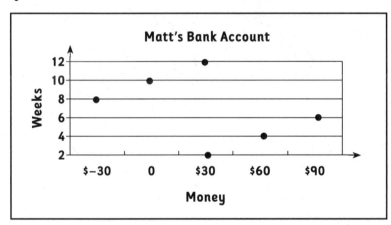

1. Between which weeks does Matt buy the game? _____

2. How many weeks does he babysit before buying the game? _____

3. Explain why Matt's bank account goes to having negative money.

_____

_____

_____

mBook Reinforce Understanding
Use the mBook *Study Guide* to review lesson concepts.

Unit 8

Name _____ Date _____

 Skills Maintenance
Adding Positive and Negative Numbers

Activity 1

Solve the addition problems. Sketch an arrow on the number line or
use the concept of red and black cards to help you. Remember in the
Interactive Text, red cards are pictured as gray cards.

1. −5 + 4 _____

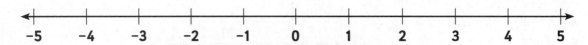

2. −6 + 6 _____

3. 11 + −9 _____

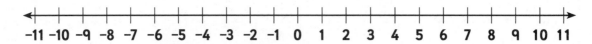

4. 3 + −4 _____

5. −7 + −9 _____

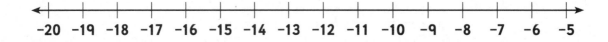

Name _____ Date _____

Apply Skills
Subtracting Positive Integers

Activity 1

Rewrite each subtraction problem as addition by adding the opposite number. You may use cards or sketch number lines to help you.

Note: In the *Interactive Text*, red cards are gray cards.

Model	5 − 7 We rewrite this problem as 5 + −7 We use cards to find the answer. There are two gray cards left. The answer is −2.

1. 6 − 1 _____   Rewrite the problem. _____

2. 2 − 5 _____   Rewrite the problem. _____

3. 5 − 4 _____   Rewrite the problem. _____

4. 3 − 3 _____   Rewrite the problem. _____

5. 2 − 3 _____   Rewrite the problem. _____

mBook Reinforce Understanding
Use the mBook *Study Guide* to review lesson concepts.

Name _____ Date _____

Skills Maintenance
Adding the Opposite

Activity 1

Give the opposite number for each of the numbers.

1. What is the opposite of −10? _____

2. What is the opposite of 5? _____

3. What is the opposite of −199? _____

4. What is the opposite of 47? _____

5. What is the opposite of −507? _____

Activity 2

Rewrite the subtraction problems as addition problems by adding the opposite number. Then solve.

1. $4 - 3$ _____

2. $7 - 2$ _____

3. $0 - 5$ _____

4. $-7 - 2$ _____

5. $-8 - 8$ _____

6. $7 - 9$ _____

Name _____ Date _____

%÷ Apply Skills
Subtracting Integers

Activity 1

Rewrite each subtraction problem as an addition problem by adding the opposite number. Circle the number that you are finding the opposite of. Tell what the opposite number is. Then solve.

1. $6 - 4$ The opposite of _____ is _____ .

   The addition problem is _____ + _____ = _____ .

2. $-8 - -3$ The opposite of _____ is _____ .

   The addition problem is _____ + _____ = _____ .

3. $7 - 8$ The opposite of _____ is _____ .

   The addition problem is _____ + _____ = _____ .

4. $5 - -3$ The opposite of _____ is _____ .

   The addition problem is _____ + _____ = _____ .

Activity 2

Solve the addition and subtraction problems involving positive and negative integers. Remember to rewrite the subtraction problems as addition problems by adding the opposite number.

1. $-4 - 3$ Rewrite the problem if necessary.

   Answer _____

2. $5 + -7$ Rewrite the problem if necessary.

   Answer _____

3. $-6 - -8$ Rewrite the problem if necessary.

   Answer _____

4. $-1 + -9$ Rewrite the problem if necessary.

   Answer _____

Unit 8

Name _____ Date _____

 Problem-Solving Activity
Dot Graphs With a Grid

Use the information in the table to create a dot graph on the grid.

Trail Point	Elevation
A	50
B	49
C	45
D	35
E	16
F	7
G	−5
H	−10
I	−2
J	12

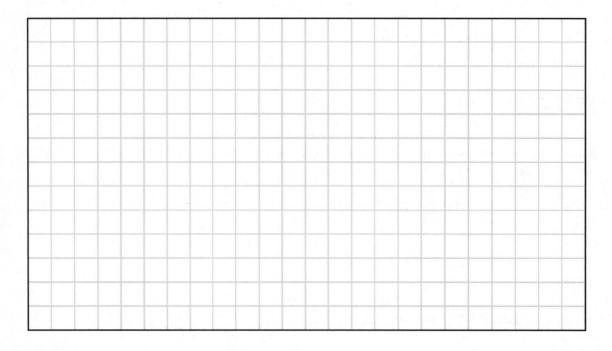

mBook Reinforce Understanding
Use the mBook *Study Guide* to review lesson concepts.

Name _____ Date _____

 Skills Maintenance
Finding Opposites

> **Activity 1**

Rewrite each subtraction problem as an addition problem by adding the opposite number. Circle the number that you are finding the opposite of. Tell what the opposite number is. Then solve.

1. $-3 - 5$ The opposite of _____ is _____ .

   The addition equation is _____ + _____ = _____ .

2. $8 - 9$ The opposite of _____ is _____ .

   The addition equation is _____ + _____ = _____ .

3. $-2 - -3$ The opposite of _____ is _____ .

   The addition equation is _____ + _____ = _____ .

4. $7 - -5$ The opposite of _____ is _____ .

   The addition equation is _____ + _____ = _____ .

Name _____ Date _____

 Apply Skills
A Mix of Addition and Subtraction

Activity 1

The Red and Black Game is a simple game that you can play with a deck of cards, paper, and a pencil. The table shows the values for the cards.

Black cards are positive and red cards are negative. The player with the highest score in each round wins that round.

Here's how to play the game: Two players have a deck of cards, paper, and a pencil. Shuffle the deck and deal five cards face down to each player. Each player turns over cards one at a time and adds the value of the cards. Use the paper and pencil to do the addition. Your turn is over when you have turned over and added all five of your cards.

Use the cards on the next page to play a practice round of the game. In the first round, you are to add the integers. In the second round, you are to subtract the integers. Show your work. Remember, red cards are gray cards in the *Interactive Text*.

Card	Value
Ace	1
2 through 10	The face value of the card
Face cards	10

Name _____ Date _____

Practice Round 1—Addition

Practice Round 2—Subtraction

Activity 2

Play the game on your own.

mBook Reinforce Understanding
Use the mBook *Study Guide* to review lesson concepts.

Name _____ Date _____

 ## Skills Maintenance
Addition and Subtraction of Positive and Negative Integers

Activity 1

Solve the addition and subtraction problems.

1. $5 + -3$ _____

2. $-4 + -7$ _____

3. $4 - -5$ _____

4. $-3 - -6$ _____

5. $2 - 8$ _____

6. $-3 + 9$ _____

7. $10 - -4$ _____

8. $2 + -10$ _____

9. $4 - 5$ _____

Name _____ Date _____

Problem-Solving Activity
Coordinate Graphs

On the coordinate graph, find the location of each of the given coordinate pairs. Place a dot at the location, and label it with its letter and the x- and y-coordinates.

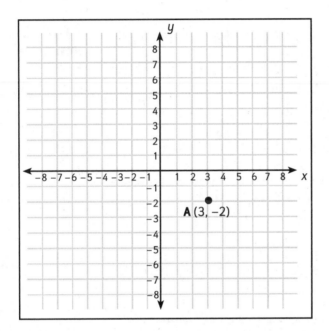

Model	Find the location of (3, −2). Place a dot at the location and label it A.

1. Find the location of (−5, 1). Place a dot at the location and label it B.

2. Find the location of (2, 4). Place a dot at the location and label it C.

3. Find the location of (−3, −4). Place a dot at the location and label it D.

4. Find the location of (5, −1). Place a dot at the location and label it E.

5. Find the location of (−1, 0). Place a dot at the location and label it F.

mBook Reinforce Understanding
Use the mBook *Study Guide* to review lesson concepts.

Name _____ Date _____

 Skills Maintenance
Addition and Subtraction of Positive and Negative Integers

Activity 1

The arrow and number line represent both an addition problem and a subtraction problem. Write both.

Model

The addition problem is <u>8</u> + <u>−3</u> = <u>5</u>.

The subtraction problem is <u>8</u> − <u>3</u> = <u>5</u>.

1.

The addition problem is _____ + _____ = _____.

The subtraction problem is _____ − _____ = _____.

2.

The addition problem is _____ + _____ = _____.

The subtraction problem is _____ − _____ = _____.

3.

The addition problem is _____ + _____ = _____.

The subtraction problem is _____ − _____ = _____.

Name _____ Date _____

Problem-Solving Activity
More Coordinate Graphs

On the coordinate graph, find the location of each of the given coordinate pairs. Place a dot at the location, and label it with its letter and the x- and y-coordinates.

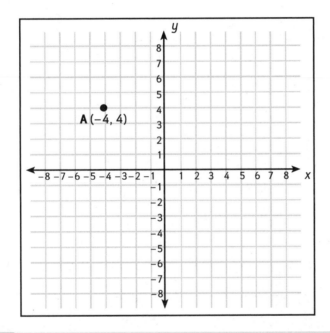

Model	Find the location of (−4, 4). Place a dot at the location and label it A

1. Find the location of (−2, 2). Place a dot at the location and label it B.

2. Find the location of (1, 3). Place a dot at the location and label it C.

3. Find the location of (−5, −6). Place a dot at the location and label it D.

4. Find the location of (7, 0). Place a dot at the location and label it E.

5. Find the location of (−1, −3). Place a dot at the location and label it F.

Unit 8

Name _____ Date _____

 Problem-Solving Activity
More Coordinate Graphs

Give the coordinate pair (*x*, *y*) that describes the location of each point on
the coordinate graph.

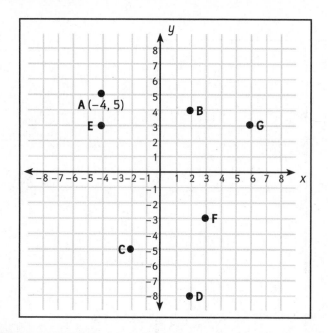

Model	A <u>(−4, 5)</u>

1. B _____   2. C _____

3. D _____   4. E _____

5. F _____   6. G _____

mBook **Reinforce Understanding**
Use the mBook *Study Guide* to review lesson concepts.

Name _____ Date _____

 ## Skills Maintenance
Adding and Subtracting Positive and Negative Integers

Activity 1

Solve.

1. −4 − −1 _____

2. 8 − 9 _____

3. 7 − −7 _____

4. −7 + 8 _____

5. 14 − 7 _____

6. −12 + −5 _____

7. −8 − 9 _____

8. −14 + 7 _____

9. 2 + −5 _____

10. −7 + −4 _____

Name _____ Date _____

 Problem-Solving Activity
Symmetry on a Coordinate Graph

Give the coordinates for each point labeled in the drawing. Then answer the questions.

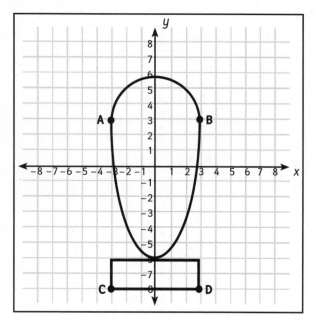

A _____

B _____

C _____

D _____

1. What do points A and B have in common? What is different about these points?

_____

_____

_____

2. What do points C and D have in common? What is different about these points?

_____

_____

_____

mBook Reinforce Understanding
Use the mBook *Study Guide* to review lesson concepts.

Name _____ Date _____

Skills Maintenance
Coordinate Graphs

Activity 1

Answer the questions about quadrants and symmetry.

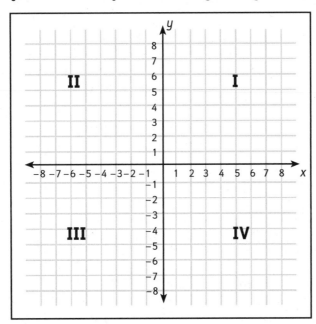

1. In which quadrant would you find the point (−2, −4)?

    (a) Quadrant I   **(b)** Quadrant II

    (c) Quadrant III   **(d)** Quadrant IV

2. In which quadrant would you find the point (3, −1)?

    (a) Quadrant I   **(b)** Quadrant II

    (c) Quadrant III   **(d)** Quadrant IV

3. Which two points are symmetrical around the *x*-axis?

    (a) (1, 2) and (2, 1)   **(b)** (−1, 2) and (−1, −2)

    (c) (−1, 2) and (1, 2)

4. Which two points are symmetrical around the *y*-axis?

    (a) (3, 4) and (3, 4)   **(b)** (3, 4) and (3, −4)

    (c) (3, 4) and (−3, 4)

Unit 8

Name _____ Date _____

%÷/<x **Apply Skills**
Working With Large Integers

Activity 1

Estimate the location of each number on the number line provided. The first one is done for you.

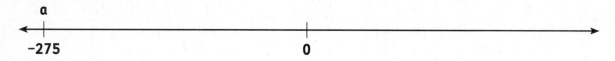

1. a = −275

2. b = −150

3. c = 100

4. d = −50

5. e = −200

6. f = 175

Activity 2

Solve the problems by using number lines, number sense, and a calculator.

1. −275 − −150

   (a) Estimate the location of the first number on the number line.

   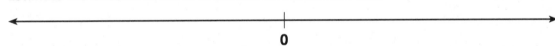

   0

   (b) If necessary, rewrite the subtraction problem as an addition problem by adding the opposite.

   _____ + _____

   (c) Where do you think your answer will fall on the number line?

   Circle one.   Positive   or   Negative

   (d) Use your calculator to solve. _____

2. −250 + 100

   (a) Estimate the location of the first number on the number line.

   ◄─────────────────────────────┼──────────────────►
   0

   (b) If necessary, rewrite the subtraction problem as an addition problem by adding the opposite.

   _____ + _____

   (c) Where do you think your answer will fall on the number line?

   Circle one.   Positive   or   Negative

   (d) Use your calculator to solve. _____

mBook **Reinforce Understanding**
Use the mBook *Study Guide* to review lesson concepts.

Name _____ Date _____

 Skills Maintenance
Large Integer Addition and Subtraction

Activity 1

Solve the addition and subtraction problems using the number lines.

1. −175 − 75 _____

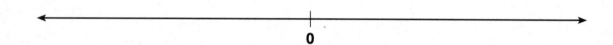

2. 300 − 400 _____

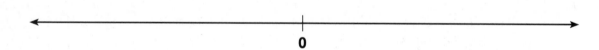

3. −800 + 300 _____

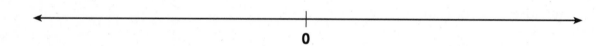

4. −500 − −300 _____

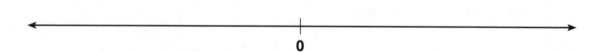

5. 700 + −800 _____

Name _____ Date _____

%÷ Apply Skills
Other Kinds of Negative Numbers

Activity 1

Solve the addition and subtraction problems.

1. $1.25 - 4.5$ _____

2. $-8.5 - -2.0$ _____

3. $15.7 + -8.6$ _____

4. $-3.2 + -4.8$ _____

5. $-22.75 + -48.25$ _____

6. $-142.05 - 85.50$ _____

Activity 2

Read the problem and determine if the business is in the black or in the red. Make a table with separate columns for income and expenses. Before you subtract expenses from profits, round your number and estimate your answer. Use a modified number line, if necessary. Then use a calculator to find if the business is in the black or in the red.

1. Ray's Music has been in business since 1982. He has CDs and DVDs. He also buys used CDs and sells them again. Ray has 4 employees, and 2 of them work part time. Ray paid his employees $7,245.23 in May. He also paid $955.10 in rent that month. He bought $125 in used CDs and $944.15 in new CDs and DVDs. Ray sold $6,935.14 in new CDs and DVDs. He also sold $875.45 in used CDs.

    How much is Ray in the black or in the red? _____

mBook Reinforce Understanding
Use the mBook *Study Guide* to review lesson concepts.

Unit 8

Name _____ Date _____

 Skills Maintenance
Addition and Subtraction With Integers

Activity 1

Solve the addition and subtraction problems.

1. $-5 + -3$ _____

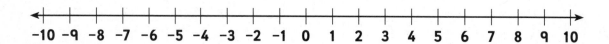

2. $4 - -6$ _____

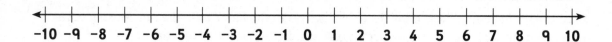

3. $2 + -5$ _____

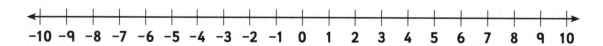

4. $-1 - 8$ _____

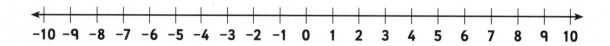

Inequalities

Activity 2

Fill in the missing inequality symbol (> or <) in the problems.

1. -1 _____ -2

2. -10 _____ -9

3. 0 _____ -1

4. 5 _____ -7

Name _____ Date _____

Unit Review
Integers

Activity 1

Solve the addition and subtraction problems.

1. 4 + −3 _____

2. 7 − 9 _____

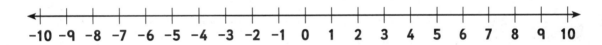

3. −4 + −3 _____

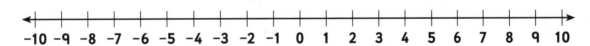

4. 8 − −2 _____

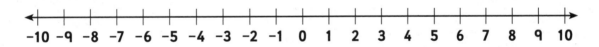

5. −3 − −5 _____

Name _____ Date _____

Activity 2

Tell if the answers are positive or negative by circling them. Do not solve the problems.

1. $4 - 8$

    Positive   or   Negative

2. $-5 - 4$

    Positive   or   Negative

3. $5 - -2$

    Positive   or   Negative

4. $-10 + 5$

    Positive   or   Negative

5. $4 + -3$

    Positive   or   Negative

6. $-5 - -8$

    Positive   or   Negative

Activity 3

Solve the addition and subtraction problems.

1. $-30 + 100$ _____

2. $67 - -22$ _____

3. $-90 - -45$ _____

4. $20 + -33$ _____

5. $72 + -32$ _____

6. $-88 - 12$ _____

7. $-50 - -72$ _____

8. $5 - -300$ _____

9. $-23 + -56$ _____

Name _____ Date _____

 Unit Review
Finding Points on a Graph

Activity 1

The dot graph shows Ty's point totals for a trivia game with 10 questions. Each correct answer was worth 5 points. Each time Ty answered incorrectly, 5 points were deducted from his score. Answer the questions using data from the graph.

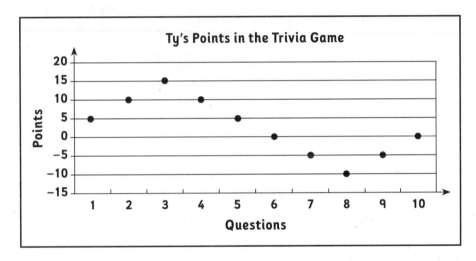

1. What was Ty's score after the first three questions?

   (a) 5

   (b) 10

   (c) 15

2. What was Ty's point total at the end of the game?

   (a) −5

   (b) 0

   (c) 10

3. How many questions did Ty answer correctly?

   (a) 5

   (b) 7

   (c) 9

4. When was Ty's score −10?

   (a) Question 4

   (b) Question 7

   (c) Question 8

Name _____ Date _____

Activity 2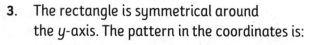

Answer the questions about the rectangle on the coordinate graph.

1. Which point has the coordinates (−3, 1)?

   (a) A

   (b) B

   (c) C

   (d) D

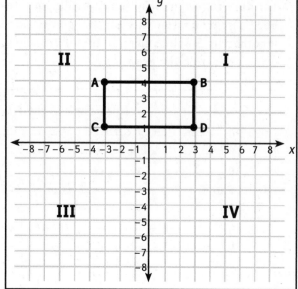

2. The rectangle is in 2 Quadrants. Which ones are they?

   (a) Quadrant I and Quadrant IV

   (b) Quadrant II and Quadrant III

   (c) Quadrant I and Quadrant II

3. The rectangle is symmetrical around the y-axis. The pattern in the coordinates is:

   (a) The Xs are positive and the Ys are negative.

   (b) The Xs are opposites and the Ys are the same.

   (c) The Xs are the same and the Ys are opposites.

4. What are the coordinates of Point B?

   (a) (3, 4)

   (b) (3, −4)

   (c) (−3, −4)

5. What point is symmetrical to Point B across the y-axis?

   (a) Point C

   (b) Point A

   (c) Point D

Name _____   Date _____

Activity 3

If a shape is symmetrical around the *y*-axis, the *x*-coordinates are opposites and the *y*-coordinates are the same. Tell the point that is symmetrical to each of the vertices.

Model	What point is symmetrical across the *y*-axis to $(3, -2)$? $\underline{(-3, -2)}$

1. What point is symmetrical across the *y*-axis to $(-1, 3)$? _____

2. What point is symmetrical across the *y*-axis to $(5, -2)$? _____

3. What point is symmetrical across the *y*-axis to $(-4, 0)$? _____

4. What point is symmetrical across the *y*-axis to $(3, -7)$? _____

5. What point is symmetrical across the *y*-axis to $(-2, -2)$? _____

6. What point is symmetrical across the *y*-axis to $(4, 4)$? _____

Unit 8

Name _____ Date _____

 Skills Maintenance
Multiplication Facts

Activity 1

Solve the multiplication facts.

1. 4 · 5 _____

2. 9 · 8 _____

3. 3 · 9 _____

4. 2 · 7 _____

5. 6 · 3 _____

6. 6 · 9 _____

7. 8 · 8 _____

8. 7 · 8 _____

9. 9 · 4 _____

Name _____ Date _____

%÷ Apply Skills
≤< x Multiplying Positive and Negative Integers

Activity 1

Multiply to solve the problems. Write the numbers on the number lines to show the problems as repeated addition.

Model

4 • −3
Use this bar to represent a unit of −3.

−12   −9   −6   −3

0

4 • −3 ___−12___

1. 3 • −2   Use this bar to represent a unit of −2.

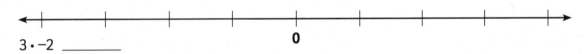

3 • −2 _____   0

2. 2 • −4   Use this bar to represent a unit of −4.

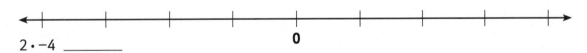

2 • −4 _____   0

3. 3 • −5   Use this bar to represent a unit of −5.

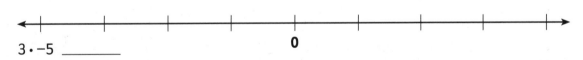

3 • −5 _____   0

Activity 2

Solve the multiplication problems.

1. 5 • −3 _____

2. 4 • −8 _____

3. 9 • −2 _____

4. 9 • −6 _____

5. 7 • −6 _____

6. 9 • −3 _____

Unit 9

Name _____ Date _____

 ## Problem-Solving Activity
Coordinate Graph Review

Today you will play a new game called the Coordinate Graph Game.

You need: 2 players, a deck of cards containing the Ace (or 1) through 9 cards, 2 different colored pens or pencils (one for each player), a coordinate graph.

Draw a point with coordinates anywhere on the coordinate graph. Label this point T, which stands for Target.

Red cards stand for negative numbers, and black cards stand for positive numbers. Each player draws a card. The player with the highest card starts.

The point of the game is to make a coordinate with two cards closest to the target. You figure out which one point is closest by counting the total number of units over and up or down from your point to the target point.

The first player draws two cards. Each card can be used as a coordinate in any order. The graph below shows how the players have chosen (–5, 5) as their target point. It also shows how Player 1 can use a 2 of hearts and a 4 of spades that she has drawn. These cards are equal to 4 and –2. The player has made the coordinate (–2, 4) because it is much closer to the target point than (4, –2) would have been. It is 1 unit up and 3 units over (or a total of 4 units) from the target point.

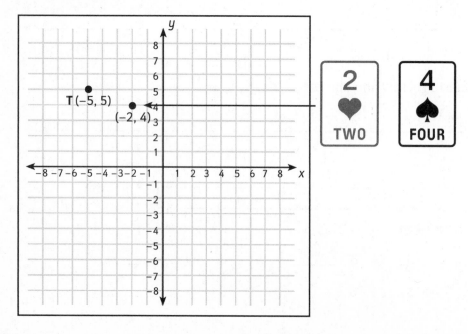

Name _____ Date _____

Player 2 draws two cards and tries to get as close to the target point as possible.

Play continues for three rounds. That means each player dots three points on the coordinate graph. The player with the closest point to the target point wins. If two points are the same distance from the target point, the game is a tie.

After you have played several rounds of the game, think about the following questions:

- How do you decide how to arrange the cards to make coordinates?

- How do you determine if two points are equally distanced from the target point?

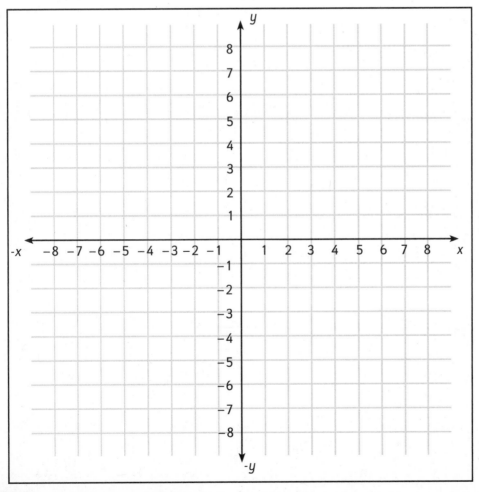

mBook Reinforce Understanding
Use the mBook *Study Guide* to review lesson concepts.

Name _____ Date _____

Skills Maintenance
Multiplying a Positive and a Negative Integer

Activity 1

Solve the problems by multiplying positive and negative integers.

1. $2 \cdot -8$ _____

2. $9 \cdot -4$ _____

3. $9 \cdot -8$ _____

4. $-2 \cdot 4$ _____

5. $2 \cdot -3$ _____

6. $-6 \cdot 6$ _____

7. $6 \cdot -8$ _____

8. $-8 \cdot 7$ _____

9. $7 \cdot -4$ _____

Name _____ Date _____

%÷ Apply Skills
≤x Multiplying Negative Integers

Activity 1

Use the multiplication rules to tell if the answers are positive or negative. Circle the answer.

1. $235 \cdot -8$ Positive   or   Negative

2. $-35 \cdot -81$ Positive   or   Negative

3. $207 \cdot 9$ Positive   or   Negative

4. $-415 \cdot -10$ Positive   or   Negative

5. $5 \cdot -329$ Positive   or   Negative

6. $-287 \cdot 3$ Positive   or   Negative

Activity 2

Complete the multiplication problems with positive and negative integers.

1. $-2 \cdot -8 =$ _____

2. $7 \cdot$ _____ $= 56$

3. $-6 \cdot -3 =$ _____

4. $-9 \cdot 8 =$ _____

5. $-4 \cdot$ _____ $= 28$

6. _____ $\cdot 5 = -25$

7. $-6 \cdot$ _____ $= 36$

8. $4 \cdot$ _____ $= 36$

9. _____ $\cdot 9 = -54$

10. $-2 \cdot -3 =$ _____

11. _____ $\cdot -4 = -24$

12. _____ $\cdot 7 = -63$

Name _____ Date _____

Problem-Solving Activity
Drawing Shapes on Coordinate Graphs

Now it's your turn to use coordinates to draw a shape. Draw the trapezoid on the coordinate graph. Start the drawing by placing the coordinates on the graph. Then connect the points to make the shape.

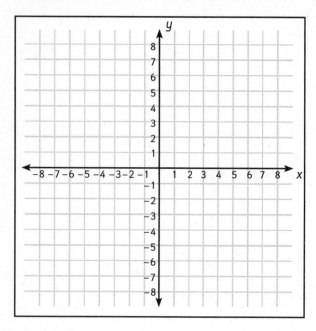

A: (0, 1)   B: (1, 5)

C: (4, 5)   D: (6, 1)

mBook **Reinforce Understanding**
Use the mBook *Study Guide* to review lesson concepts.

Name _____ Date _____

Skills Maintenance
Multiplying Positive and Negative Integers

Activity 1

Decide if the answer will be positive or negative. Circle the answer.

1. −298 · −73   Positive   or   Negative

2. −90 · 77   Positive   or   Negative

3. 5,043 · 7   Positive   or   Negative

4. 832 · −43   Positive   or   Negative

5. −7,663 · −3,874   Positive   or   Negative

6. −9,999 · 1   Positive   or   Negative

7. −80 · −67   Positive   or   Negative

8. 432 · −20   Positive   or   Negative

9. 1,029 · 341   Positive   or   Negative

10. −33 · −10   Positive   or   Negative

Name _____ Date _____

Problem-Solving Activity
Line Segments on a Graph

Create line segments on the graph based on the Starting Segment coordinates. Then add or subtract the number from the coordinate specified in the problem.

Before you fill in the Ending Segment table, see if you can sketch what the new line segment will look like. Your job is to make predictions about the new line based on the numbers in the table.

Problem 1

Starting Segment	
End Points	Coordinates
A	(6, 2)
B	(8, 6)

Add 3 to each *y*-coordinate.

Ending Segment	
End Points	Coordinates
A'	
B'	

Problem 1

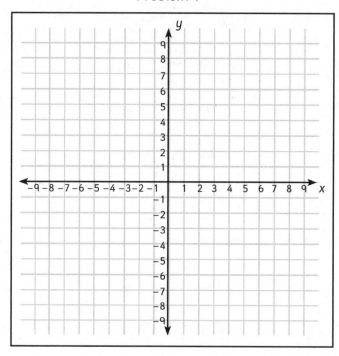

Name _____ Date _____

Problem 2

Starting Segment	
End Points	Coordinates
L	(2, 1)
M	(2, 7)

Subtract 5 from each
x-coordinate.

Ending Segment	
End Points	Coordinates
L'	
M'	

Problem 2

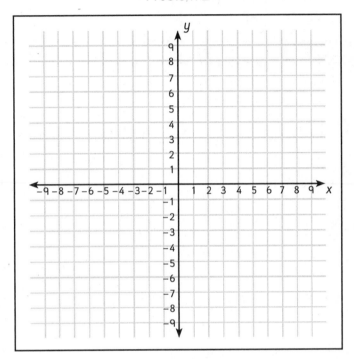

Problem 3

Starting Segment	
End Points	Coordinates
X	(−8, 4)
Y	(−4, 4)

Add 10 to each *x*-coordinate.

Ending Segment	
End Points	Coordinates
X'	
Y'	

Problem 3

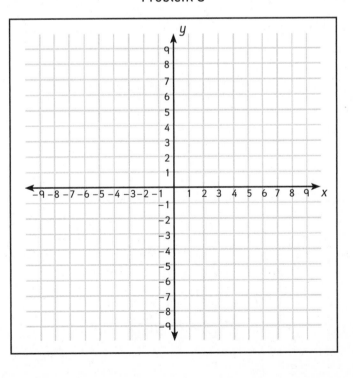

mBook **Reinforce Understanding**
Use the mBook *Study Guide* to review lesson concepts.

Unit 9

Name _____ Date _____

 Skills Maintenance
Basic Division Facts

Activity 1

Solve the basic division facts.

1.   16 ÷ 2 _____

2.   6)‾2‾4‾

3. $\frac{28}{7}$ _____

4.   72 ÷ 9 _____

5.   32 ÷ 8 _____

6.   9)‾5‾4‾

7. $\frac{36}{6}$ _____

8.   35 ÷ 5 _____

Name _____ Date _____

Apply Skills
Dividing Negative Numbers

Activity 1

Solve the division problems with positive and negative numbers. Watch the signs carefully and use the PASS rules.

1. $-72 \div 8$ _____

2. $-8\overline{)-64}$

3. $-\dfrac{36}{4}$ _____

4. $27 \div -9$ _____

5. $-32 \div -4$ _____

6. $-5\overline{)30}$

7. $\dfrac{-18}{-3}$ _____

8. $-25 \div -5$ _____

Activity 2

Decide whether the answer to each division problem is positive or negative. Circle the answer.

1. $-400 \div 8$ Positive   or   Negative

2. $-36\overline{)-72}$ Positive   or   Negative

3. $-\dfrac{35}{5}$ Positive   or   Negative

4. $-864 \div -4$ Positive   or   Negative

5. $7\overline{)-490}$ Positive   or   Negative

6. $\dfrac{60}{-10}$ Positive   or   Negative

Name _____ Date _____

 ## Problem-Solving Activity
Translating Two-Dimensional Shapes

In this exercise, you are given coordinates for a shape that is shown on a coordinate graph. Figure out how much you add or subtract to move the shape to a different quadrant. Make sure that the entire shape ends up in the new quadrant. Begin by filling in the second table of coordinates, then draw the translated shape. Be sure to label the vertices.

Problem 1

Starting Segment	
Vertices	Coordinates
A	(3, -2)
B	(8, -2)
C	(8, -5)
D	(3, -5)

Move the rectangle from Quadrant IV to Quadrant III.

Ending Segment	
Vertices	Coordinates
A'	
B'	
C'	
D'	

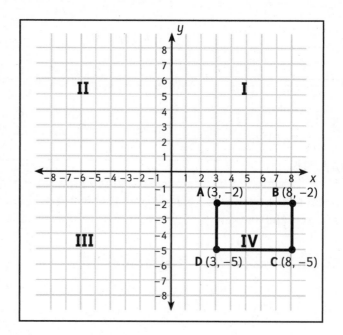

Name _____ Date _____

Problem 2

Starting Segment	
Vertices	Coordinates
A	(-5, 8)
B	(-3, 5)
C	(-5, 2)
D	(-7, 5)

Move the rhombus from Quadrant II to Quadrant I.

Ending Segment	
Vertices	Coordinates
A'	
B'	
C'	
D'	

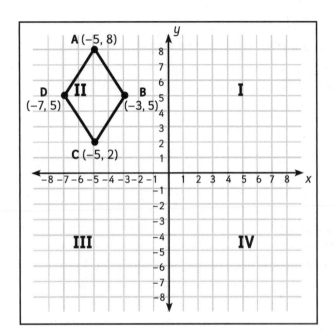

mBook Reinforce Understanding
Use the mBook *Study Guide* to review lesson concepts.

Unit 9 • Lesson 4   **333**

Name _____ Date _____

Skills Maintenance
Operations With Positive and Negative Integers

Activity 1

Complete the mix of multiplication and division problems.

1. $-12 \div 3$ _____

2. $-8 \cdot$ _____ -24

3. $-8\overline{)-56}$

4. $\dfrac{21}{-7}$ _____

5. $21 \div -7$ _____

6. _____ $\cdot 9 = 45$

Activity 2

Tell the coordinates of the reflected line segments.

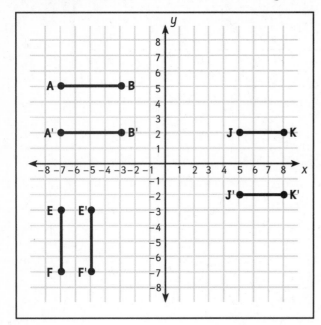

1. $\overline{AB}$ = (_____ , _____) and (_____ , _____)

   $\overline{A'B'}$ = (_____ , _____) and (_____ , _____)

2. $\overline{EF}$ = (_____ , _____) and (_____ , _____)

   $\overline{E'F'}$ = (_____ , _____) and (_____ , _____)

3. $\overline{JK}$ = (_____ , _____) and (_____ , _____)

   $\overline{J'K'}$ = (_____ , _____) and (_____ , _____)

Name _____ Date _____

Problem-Solving Activity
Absolute Value

Evaluate the absolute values.

1. $|-5|$ _____
2. $|10|$ _____
3. $|-4|$ _____

4. $|-8|$ _____
5. $|6|$ _____
6. $|-3|$ _____

Now use the concept of absolute value to translate line segments on the graph.

7. $\overline{AB}$ $|8|$ _____

8. $\overline{XY}$ $|-4|$ _____

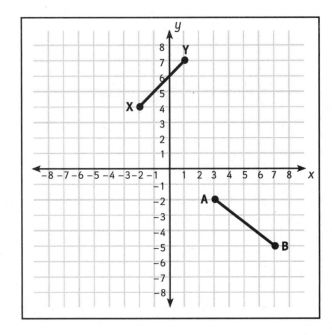

mBook Reinforce Understanding
Use the mBook *Study Guide* to review lesson concepts.

Unit 9 • Lesson 5 **335**

Unit 9

Name _____ Date _____

 ## Skills Maintenance
Addition and Subtraction With Integers

Activity 1

Solve the addition and subtraction problems.

1. $7 + -9$ _____

2. $-3 - -5$ _____

3. $-5 - 7$ _____

4. $1 - 9$ _____

5. $-6 + 24$ _____

6. $5 - -3$ _____

7. $8 + -2$ _____

8. $-3 + -9 =$ _____

Coordinates

Activity 2

Find the coordinates of the points on the grid.

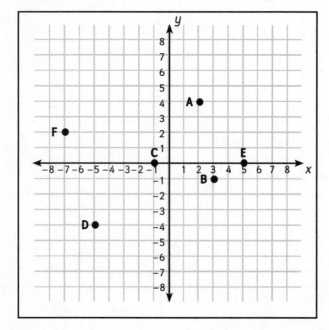

A _____   B _____

C _____   D _____

E _____   F _____

Name _____ Date _____

%÷ Apply Skills
Keeping It Straight: Integer Operations

Activity 1

Solve each of the problems using the chart on page 656 of the *Student Text*.

1. −3 · −4

    Step 1: What is the operation?

    Step 2: Circle the negative signs.

    Step 3: Remember the rule.

    Answer _____

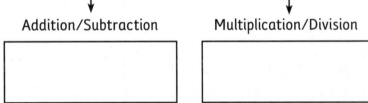

Rewrite the problem here.

Addition/Subtraction   Multiplication/Division

Rule: Subtraction is   Rule: PASS
adding the opposite.

2. −25 ÷ 5

    Step 1: What is the operation?

    Step 2: Circle the negative signs.

    Step 3: Remember the rule.

    Answer _____

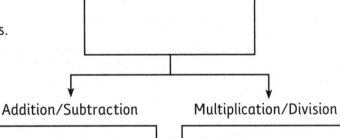

Rewrite the problem here.

Addition/Subtraction   Multiplication/Division

Rule: Subtraction is   Rule: PASS
adding the opposite.

Name _____ Date _____

3. −3 + 7

Step 1: What is the operation?

Step 2: Circle the negative signs.

Step 3: Remember the rule.

Answer _____

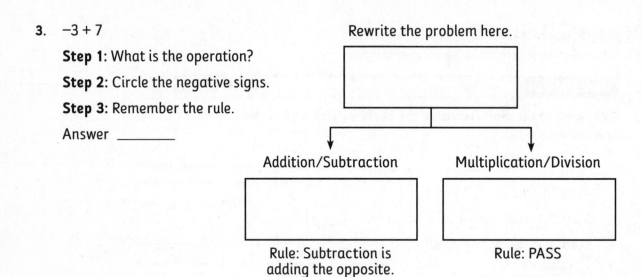

Rewrite the problem here.

Addition/Subtraction

Rule: Subtraction is adding the opposite.

Multiplication/Division

Rule: PASS

4. −8 − 5

Step 1: What is the operation?

Step 2: Circle the negative signs.

Step 3: Remember the rule.

Answer _____

Rewrite the problem here.

Addition/Subtraction

Rule: Subtraction is adding the opposite.

Multiplication/Division

Rule: PASS

mBook Reinforce Understanding

Use the mBook *Study Guide* to review lesson concepts.

Name _____ Date _____

Skills Maintenance
Integer Operations

Activity 1

Solve the mix of problems involving addition, subtraction, multiplication, and division of positive and negative numbers.

1. $-1 + -3$ _____

2. $-32 \div -4$ _____

3. $-4 \cdot -4$ _____

4. $1 - 8$ _____

5. $-7 \cdot 6$ _____

6. $-4 + -4$ _____

7. $-40 \div 8$ _____

8. $-50 - -30$ _____

Unit 9

Name _____ Date _____

Problem-Solving Activity
Reflecting Line Segments

In this exercise, you are given a starting table of coordinates. You will reflect a line segment based on those coordinates. You need to use an opposite to make a change in one of the coordinates. Before you fill in the second table of coordinates, see if you can sketch what the new line segment will look like on the graph. Your job is to make predictions about the new line based on the numbers in the second table.

Problem 1

Starting Segment	
End Points	Coordinates
A	(5, −2)
B	(7, −4)

Reflect the line segments using the opposites for the *y*-coordinate.

Ending Segment	
End Points	Coordinates
A'	
B'	

Problem 1

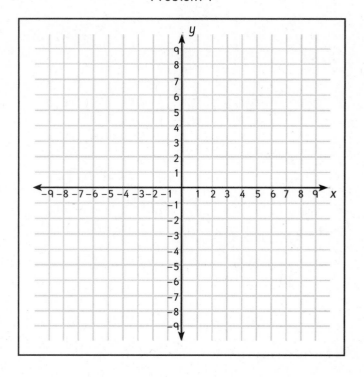

Name _____ Date _____

Problem 2

Starting Segment	
End Points	Coordinates
C	(4, −5)
D	(4, −9)

Reflect the line segments using the opposites for the x-coordinate.

Ending Segment	
End Points	Coordinates
C'	
D'	

Problem 2

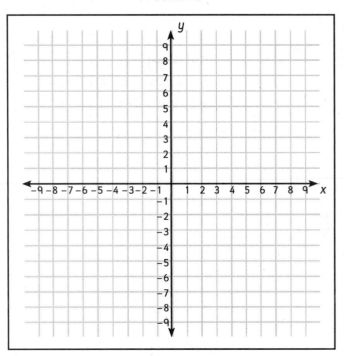

Problem 3

Starting Segment	
End Points	Coordinates
L	(−2, 7)
K	(2, 7)

Reflect the line segments using the opposites for the y-coordinate.

Ending Segment	
End Points	Coordinates
L'	
K'	

Problem 3

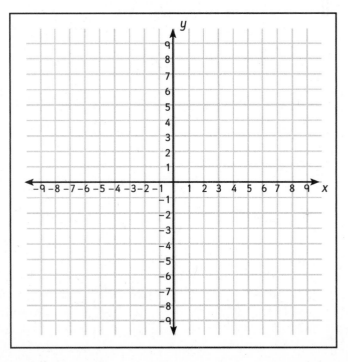

mBook **Reinforce Understanding**
Use the mBook *Study Guide* to review lesson concepts.

Name _____ Date _____

 Skills Maintenance
Mixed Integer Operations

Activity 1

Solve the problems involving addition, subtraction, multiplication, and division of positive and negative integers.

1. $-9 + 7$ _____

2. $56 \div -8$ _____

3. $-6 \cdot -8$ _____

4. $-9 - 8$ _____

5. $4 \cdot -1$ _____

6. $-4 + 18$ _____

7. $-80 \div -5$ _____

8. $-16 - -17$ _____

9. $4 + -100$ _____

Name _____ Date _____

 Problem-Solving Activity
Translations Versus Reflections

In today's exercise, you look at two sets of tables and two shapes on a coordinate graph. Look carefully at the tables and see what is happening to the different vertices. Ask yourself, "Is a number being added to or subtracted from a coordinate? If so, it is a translation?" Also ask, "Is the new coordinate in the second table an opposite? If so, it is a reflection?"

1. Begin by imagining what the second shape looks like. Think about its location on the graph and if it is a translation or a reflection.

2. Next draw the shape using the coordinates in the second table and label the vertices. Use the drawing to decide if you were right—was it a translation or a reflection? _____

Shape 1

Starting Points	
End Points	Coordinates
A	(−5, 7)
B	(−1, 7)
C	(−3, 4)
D	(−7, 4)

Shape 2

Ending Points	
End Points	Coordinates
A'	(2, 7)
B'	(6, 7)
C'	(4, 4)
D'	(0, 4)

Unit 9

Name _____   Date _____

Shape 1

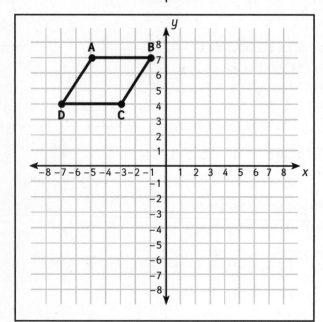

Shape 2

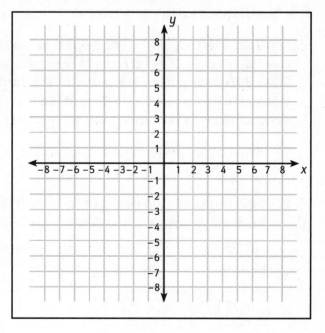

mBook Reinforce Understanding
Use the mBook *Study Guide* to review lesson concepts.

Name _____ Date _____

Skills Maintenance
Integer Operations

Activity 1

Solve the problems. Do not use a calculator.

1. $-1 + 7$ _____

2. $16 \div -8$ _____

3. $-2 \cdot -4$ _____

4. $-3 - 2$ _____

5. $5 \cdot -9$ _____

6. $-4 + -4$ _____

Translations and Reflections

Activity 2

Tell whether the shape has been translated or reflected. Circle the correct answer.

1. 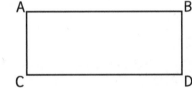   Translated or Reflected

2.    Translated or Reflected

3. 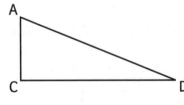   Translated or Reflected

4. 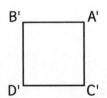   Translated or Reflected

Name _____ Date _____

%÷ Apply Skills
Patterns With Integers

Activity 1

Answer the questions about prime, odd, even, and consecutive numbers.

1. What is the next consecutive even number after 10?

   a. 8   b. 12   c. 11   d. 14

2. What is the next consecutive odd number after 29?

   a. 30   b. 31   c. 27   d. 25

3. Which of the following numbers are prime numbers?

   a. 6   b. 4   c. 8   d. 2

4. Which of the following numbers is odd and prime?

   a. 2   b. 25   c. 5   d. 27

Activity 2

Refer to the table of integers and their properties on page 670 of the
Student Text. List the properties of these numbers.

1. −20

   Prime? _____   Even? _____   Odd? _____

   What is the next consecutive number? _____

   What is the next consecutive even or odd number? _____

2. 11

   Prime? _____   Even? _____   Odd? _____

   What is the next consecutive number? _____

   What is the next consecutive even or odd number? _____

mBook Reinforce Understanding
Use the mBook *Study Guide* to review lesson concepts.

Name _____ Date _____

Skills Maintenance
Absolute Values

Activity 1

Solve the problems involving absolute values.

1. $3 + |5|$ _____

2. $-4 + |-4|$ _____

3. $7 + |8|$ _____

4. $-8 + |8|$ _____

5. $-12 - |-10|$ _____

6. $12 \div |-3|$ _____

7. $3 \cdot |-5|$ _____

8. $100 - |-98|$ _____

Unit 9

Name _____ Date _____

 Unit Review
Operations on Integers

Activity 1

Solve the mix of addition, subtraction, multiplication, and division problems with integers.

1. $100 \div -10$ _____

2. $-300 \cdot -50$ _____

3. $-27 - 4$ _____

4. $8 + 10$ _____

5. $-70 + 45$ _____

6. $40 \cdot -3$ _____

7. $-44 \div -11$ _____

8. $16 + -8$ _____

Activity 2

Find the missing integer in each equation.

1. $16 \div -4 =$ _____

2. _____ $\cdot -5 = -20$

3. $10 -$ _____ $= 30$

4. $30 \div$ _____ $= 6$

5. _____ $+ -15 = -5$

6. $-30 \cdot -5 =$ _____

7. $35 \div$ _____ $= 5$

8. _____ $+ 40 = -3$

Name _____ Date _____

Unit Review
Coordinate Graphs and Transformations

Activity 1

Follow the directions and draw lines and line segments on the graph.

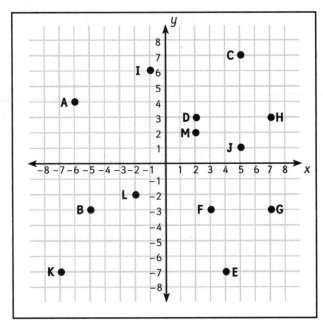

1. Draw line $\overleftrightarrow{AB}$.

2. Draw line segment $\overline{FG}$.

3. Draw line $\overleftrightarrow{CJ}$.

4. Draw line segment $\overline{KE}$.

5. Draw line segment $\overline{DH}$.

6. Draw line $\overleftrightarrow{LM}$.

Name _____ Date _____

Activity 2

Begin by filling in the second table of coordinates, and then draw the translated shape. Be sure to label the vertices.

Starting Points	
Vertices	**Coordinates**
A	(4, 7)
B	(8, 7)
C	(10, 2)
D	(2, 2)

Move the trapezoid from Quadrant I to Quadrant IV.

Ending Points	
Vertices	**Coordinates**
A'	
B'	
C'	
D'	

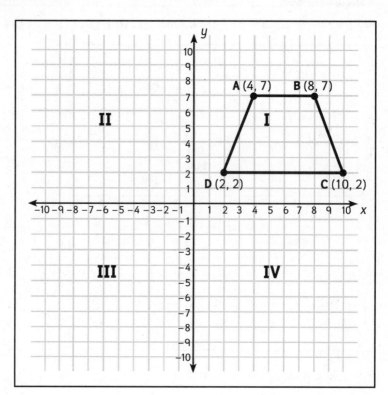

Name _____ Date _____

Activity 3

Follow the directions to reflect line segments.

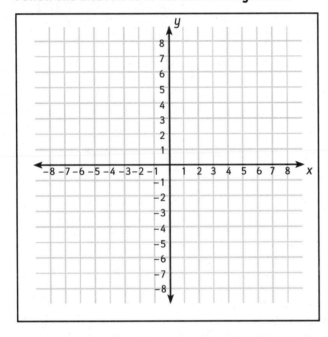

1. Use a protractor and draw a 45-degree angle from the origin point to point (6, 6). Call the line segment $\overline{AB}$.

2. Reflect $\overline{AB}$ over the *x*-axis and draw a line segment called $\overline{CD}$.

3. What are the coordinates of the endpoints of $\overline{CD}$? _____

4. Describe patterns in the endpoints.

_____

_____

_____

_____

mBook **Reinforce Understanding**
Use the mBook *Study Guide* to review lesson concepts.

Unit 9